Cambridge checkp•int

THIRD EDITION

Lower Secondary

English

7

John Reynolds

HODDER
EDUCATION
AN HACHETTE UK COMPANY

The questions, example answers and comments that appear in this book were written by the author. In an examination, the way marks would be awarded to answers like these may be different.

The publishers would like to thank the following for permission to reproduce copyright material:

Text credits

[to come]

Photo credits

[to come]

Acknowledgements

Every effort has been made to trace all copyright holders, but if any have been inadvertently overlooked, the Publishers will be pleased to make the necessary arrangements at the first opportunity.

Although every effort has been made to ensure that website addresses are correct at time of going to press, Hodder Education cannot be held responsible for the content of any website mentioned in this book. It is sometimes possible to find a relocated web page by typing in the address of the home page for a website in the URL window of your browser.

Hachette UK's policy is to use papers that are natural, renewable and recyclable products and made from wood grown in well-managed forests and other controlled sources. The logging and manufacturing processes are expected to conform to the environmental regulations of the country of origin.

Orders: please contact Hachette UK Distribution, Hely Hutchinson Centre, Milton Road, Didcot, Oxfordshire, OX11 7HH. Telephone: +44 (0)1235 827827. Email education@hachette.co.uk Lines are open from 9 a.m. to 5 p.m., Monday to Friday.

ISBN: 978 1 3983 0016 3

© John Reynolds 2021

First published in 2011

This edition published in 2021 by

Hodder Education,

An Hachette UK Company

Carmelite House

50 Victoria Embankment

London EC4Y 0DZ

www.hoddereducation.com

Impression number 10 9 8 7 6 5 4 3 2 1

Year 2025 2024 2023 2022 2021

Cover photo

Illustrations by Oxford Designers and Illustrators and Abigael Cassell

Typeset by Ian Foulis Design, Saltash, Cornwall

Printed in

A catalogue record for this title is available from the British Library.

Contents

The reading cycle

Follow these three steps to read actively.

1 **Before reading**

It may sound silly to prepare your brain to read a text, but knowing what the text type or genre is and what subject you are reading about helps you to comprehend what you read and to make connections to past learning and/or experiences.

- Look for clues about the text type or genre.
- Read the title and subtitle to find out what the text is about.
- Use skimming and scanning techniques to look for:
  - the layout of the text
  - heading levels and/or numbering of headings or subheadings
  - emphasis given through the use of different colours, key words, italics or bold
  - artwork, illustrations and/or photographs and their captions
  - graphics and graphs, diagrams, charts or maps
  - key words or specific details.

2 **During reading**

These activities will help you to analyse the structure and language features in more detail.

- Use the Word attack skills boxes to work out the meaning of words using contextual clues, the word families they are from, the morphology or root of the words.
- Ask questions while you read. Use the questions that appear alongside the texts.
- Make notes of main and supporting ideas.
- Visualise what is being described (particularly in descriptive writing).
- Pay attention to the way the creator of the text has used language and grammar to enhance the meaning in texts and to create effects.

3 **After reading**

These activities will help you to understand the meaning of the text.

- Think about the purpose and audience of the text. What was it supposed to do? Who was it written for?
- Evaluate the impact of the text on you. What is your opinion of the text?
- Evaluate and discuss different interpretations of the text.
- Think about texts that are similar to, or contrast with, the text.
- Exercise critical language awareness:
  - Distinguish between facts and opinions.
  - Compare direct (explicit) and implied (implicit) information and meaning.
  - Determine the social, political and cultural background of texts.
  - Identify emotive and manipulative language such as stereotyping and bias.

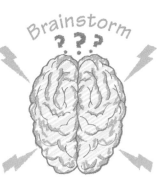

The writing cycle

1 Generate ideas by brainstorming, by writing your ideas on paper or talking with others or doing research. Think about:
   - your audience – who will read your work? Who is your text for?
   - the intended purpose of your writing – is it to entertain, inform, persuade or a combination of those things?
   - the writing features you will use to suit the text type or genre.

2 Organise your ideas by planning your writing.
   - Use different planning methods to shape your ideas, such as a mind map, a storyboard or an online template.

3 Write a draft. Think about:
   - the tone and register (formal or informal) you should use (see page 30)
   - developing distinctive voices for your characters (see page 43).

4 Revise your draft. Think about:
   - the types of sentences you could use: simple (page 44), compound (page 44), complex (page 44) or compound-complex sentences (page 99) and using different types of sentences to avoid monotony
   - the range of punctuation you could use: ellipses (page 118), colons (page 6), semi-colons (page 137) or dashes (page 6).
   - using appropriate connectives or beginning sentences with interesting connectives (page 124)
   - the range of language you could use to make your writing more interesting, such as using better adjectives (page 40) or adverbs (page 49).

5 Edit your writing.
   - Evaluate your writing by checking your language, grammar, spelling and the structure of your writing.
   - Ask a partner to read your writing and do the same.
   - Correct any mistakes.

6 Proofread your writing.
   - Rewrite or type your work. Think about different layouts and decide which one will best suit your purpose: handwritten, printed or onscreen.
   - Read through your work carefully to make sure that you have corrected all your mistakes.

7 Present your writing.

How to use this book

Spotlight on
These boxes ask you to think about specific aspects of the text, such as purpose, audience, historical context and theme.

WORD ATTACK SKILLS
These boxes ask you to look at vocabulary and language in context. This includes working out the meaning of unfamiliar words, looking at a writer's choice of language and discussing linguistic and literary techniques.

HINT
These boxes guide you to think about specific things.

The **chapter opener** pages at the beginning of each chapter give you a snapshot of all the exciting things you will do in the chapter and introduce the new topic with a 'Let's talk' activity.

Author, poet or playwright

These boxes provide extra information about the creators of texts. This is often useful when a text has been created in a particular social, historical or political context.

KEY WORDS
These boxes explain all the literary and grammar terms. The key words are repeated in the glossary pages at the back of the book for easy revision.

LET'S TALK
These activities offer opportunities to discuss the content in pairs, groups or as a class.

Spelling

These boxes encourage you to think about the spelling rules and patterns you have learned in previous stages.

Activity 1.4

These boxes allow you to explore and practise skills in pairs or groups.

EXERCISE
These boxes allow you to practise and consolidate skills on your own.

 These icons show you where content is related to another subject, such as maths or science.

THINK ABOUT
These boxes ask questions for you to think about as you read through the texts. You may prefer to try answering these on your second or third reading or after attempting the activities or extracts.

The **Reviewing** section at the end of each chapter lets you evaluate the texts you have read, suggests similar or contrasting texts for further reading and asks you to reflect on your learning in the chapter.

Reading

★ Advertisements
★ Tourist guides
★ Timetables
★ Sport rules
★ Online encyclopedias
★ Advice columns

Speaking and listening

★ Listening for factual information
★ Discussing recipes and visual texts
★ Giving clear information

IS THAT A FACT?

Writing

★ Instructions on how to make a box kite
★ Information brochure about a theme park
★ Using fast, accurate handwriting to make notes

Key skills

★ Word families
★ Paragraphs and topic sentences
★ Punctuation: dashes, colons and brackets
★ Bias

LET'S TALK

There are texts all around us, from advertising billboards to the destination indicator boards on local buses, from direction signs at road junctions to the menu selections on display in restaurant windows.

■ What is the function or purpose of these texts?

■ What are the features of a good factual text?

■ Do you think that factual texts are easier to write than fiction ones? Why do you say so?

Reading

Writing that gives factual information

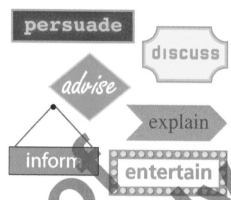

Writers convey **factual information** in different ways and for different purposes. This chapter is about how writers use language to give information and instructions, and how they describe, advise and entertain – and sometimes show bias. You will explore the information in advertisements, recipes, timetables, brochures and encyclopedias. You will read an advice column and an information text designed to entertain. You will also look at how writers organise their texts to provide this information clearly.

Spotlight on: purpose
When you read a text, always first consider what its purpose is. Why was it written?

WORD ATTACK SKILLS
Discuss what the highlighted words in the text mean and how you pronounce them.

KEY WORDS
factual information information that is accurate, true and can be checked
purpose the reason or intention for writing the piece, e.g. to amuse, to inform, to entertain

Extract: Advertisement

- Three-bedroom townhouse
- 10 m² living room
- Dining room with **parquet** floor
- Original wooden staircase
- Good size bathroom with shower
- Fireplace in main bedroom
- Attic space – potential for further bedroom
- Cellar
- Broadband connection, electricity and gas
- Close to local **amenities** and golf course
- Station/airport less than 30 minutes' drive

EXTENSION

The advertisement you have read gives information but it does not use language to attempt to persuade the reader. Work in a group and discuss what you could add to the advertisement to make the house seem more attractive.

LET'S TALK

1. Do you think the description of the house in the advertisement gives enough information to someone who might be interested in buying it? Think about the **purpose** of the text before you answer. Is there any information that could be added?
2. Discuss the layout of the advertisement. What punctuation has the writer used? Why? What do you notice about the length of the phrases? Is this useful for the reader? Do you have any other suggestions about how this text could be organised?

Activity 1.1

Work in a pair and write your own advertisement for a house or apartment that you would like to buy. Give at least 10 pieces of factual information about the house. Consider how you can present the text to make it easy to read. Punctuation is important, so think about how you will use it.

Listening

Listening for factual information

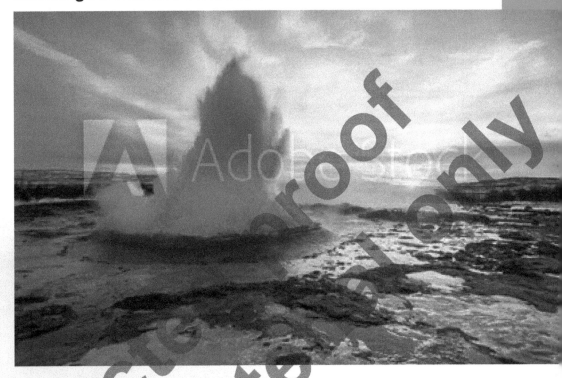

Factual texts often have numbers, dates and they use precise vocabulary. Make a note of any of these that you think are important as you listen to the text about geysers.

▶ Geysers throw up jets of hot water at regular intervals

WORD ATTACK SKILLS

You will have heard these words in the text:

✔ dormant
✔ prone
✔ fissures

Listen to the text again and discuss the meanings of these words with a partner.

KEY WORD

paragraph a group of closely related sentences that develop a central idea

HINT

You will have to write quickly while you are listening. Make sure that your notes are clear, accurate and easy to read. If your notes are not precise or easy to read, you could make errors in your paragraph.

Activity 1.2

A geyser is a hole in the ground from which hot water and steam burst out at irregular intervals. Look at the photograph.

Work in a small group and quickly describe what you think you would experience if you saw a real one. What would you see, hear, and feel?

Listen to a text about geysers in Iceland.

LET'S TALK

1 Where could you read more about geysers in Iceland?
2 What can make a dormant geyser erupt again? Why?
3 How would you know when a geyser was about to erupt?

EXERCISE 1.1

Look at the first notes you made, then listen to the text again. Write down five facts about geysers in Iceland from this text. Write one short **paragraph** using these facts. Then, read and evaluate the notes your partner made. You could use this checklist:

● Was the handwriting clear and easy to read?
● Did your partner cover all the main ideas in the time available?
● Were the notes short, with clear meanings?

3

Spotlight on: encyclopedias

The purpose of an encyclopedia is to provide accurate factual information on a wide range of topics.

LET'S TALK

After you have read the text about Serena Williams, talk about the features of this type of information text.

1 Look at the way the text is organised.
- Some of the text is in bold print. Why?
- Why is some of the information given in point form under a heading?

2 What can you say about the language?
- Which **verb** tenses are used?
- Are the sentences long or short?
- Are there any similes or other literary devices?

KEY WORD

verb a word that describes an action

Reading

An online encyclopedia

Read this text about a world-class tennis player by yourself.

Extract: Serena Williams

Serena Jameka Williams was born on 26 September 1981 in Saginaw, Michigan in the USA. She is a professional tennis player who has spent much of her career ranked world number one in **singles** and world number one in **doubles** with her sister (Venus Williams). She first became world number one on 8 July 2002. **Ranked** world number one by the Women's Tennis Association (WTA) eight times, she is considered one of the greatest champions ever. In 2012 she won Olympic Gold Medals both in the women's singles and also in the doubles competition in which she was partnered by her sister Venus Williams. She has won 39 Grand Slam titles in singles, women's doubles and **mixed doubles** as well as four Olympic gold medals.

Vital statistics

Height: 5' 9" (1.75 m) *Pro since*: September 1995

Plays: Right-handed (two-handed backhand)

Activity 1.3

In a pair, find a subject or person that you and your partner are both interested in.

Discuss what information you would expect to find in an encyclopedia entry about your subject.

Discuss what information you would expect to find in an opinion piece like a newspaper article or a blog about your subject.

3 Find an encyclopedia entry and an opinion piece about your subject.
a Review and discuss the information in each text.
b Take one text each and quickly make notes about the main ideas in each text. Spend 5–8 minutes making the notes.

Discuss the differences in the information and how it is presented.

Which text did you enjoy the most? Can you say why?

WORD ATTACK SKILLS

Some of the vocabulary is very specific to the world of tennis.

Do you understand what these words mean?
- ✔ singles
- ✔ doubles
- ✔ ranked
- ✔ mixed doubles

A tourist guide

Activity 1.4

1 Look at the following text quickly and write down in one sentence what you think it is about.
2 Work in a pair.
   a Discuss the purpose of this text. Who will read the text (who is the **audience**)? Will you find facts or opinions in this text?
   b Look at and comment on the way the text is organised. Are the headings useful? Is the text organised in sections or paragraphs? What punctuation has been used?
3 Read the brochure in detail.

Spotlight on: brochures

Brochures give factual information. Sometimes the text includes opinions too.

KEY WORD

audience people who read a text (or watch a performance)

WORD ATTACK SKILLS

Work out the meanings of the following words from the context.
✔ range
✔ soars

EXERCISE 1.2

1 At what time of the year would you plan to travel to Hong Kong? Give a reason for your answer.
2 Why might it 'come in useful' to have the name and address of your hotel written down in both Chinese and English?

Extract: Hong Kong travel tips

A visit to Hong Kong can be VERY confusing if it is your first visit. Here are some tips which will help you to prepare for your trip – and keep you safe!

Climate

There are four seasons In Hong Kong. This means that you can experience different weather conditions at different times of the year.

Winter (from mid-December to February): Temperatures may be as low as 6 °C. Many people find this a good time to visit as the weather is cool and comfortable without much rainfall.

Spring (from March to mid-May): Temperatures **range** from 18 to 27 °C. The evenings can still be cool so a light jacket or sweater would be useful.

Summer (from June to August): Temperatures rise to +30 °C, humidity **soars** and there are frequent thunderstorms.

Autumn (from September to December): Humidity falls and temperature levels are more tolerable, so this is also a very good time to visit.

Language

The official languages in Hong Kong are Chinese and English. Many people understand and speak English well, but there are also many who do not. You will find that some restaurants have their menus only in Chinese. If you are planning to use public transport or taxis, it is a good idea to ask your hotel to write the hotel's address and your destination details in Chinese, as well as in English, before you leave – and you won't get lost!

For more visitor information, you can go to the following official website: http://www.discoverhongkong.com/eng/index.jsp

Key skills

Punctuation: dashes, colons and brackets

A **dash** (–) is a short horizontal line that is placed in the middle of a line of text. Dashes are sometimes used instead of commas to give more emphasis to words or phrases in a sentence. They can also introduce an opinion.

Attic space – potential for further bedroom
Here are some tips which will help you to prepare for your trip – and keep you safe!

Dashes are also used to show ranges between numbers. (Note: there is no space before or after the dash in these examples.)

It erupts every 8–10 hours.

A **colon** (:) consists of two dots. It is used to introduce information (in a list or a paragraph sometimes). This helps to organise information and can make a text easier to read.

Winter (from mid-December to February): Temperatures may be as low as 6 °C.
There are three more ingredients we need to make the cake: flour, butter and chocolate.

Brackets can be used to separate words and numbers or to give additional information.

Because of the high temperature of volcanic rock (around 200 °C), the trapped air is heated to high temperatures.

Activity 1.5

Work in a pair and discuss how you can use punctuation to make this factual text easier to read.
Draft a revised text with a better layout. Cut some words and use dashes, colons or brackets.

The Kalahari Desert which is also known as the Kgalagadi Desert is a large area of desert and grassland in southern Africa. The area forms part of Botswana, Namibia and South Africa. The area is covered in red sand and there is little permanent surface water.

The climate of the area is harsh. There is little rainfall. The area gets between 110 and 500 millimetres per year and the temperatures in summer are very high. The total area of the desert is about 900,000 square kilometres.

The traditional inhabitants of the area are the San people. They have lived in the Kalahari for 20,000 years. They live off the land and get water from plants.

The flora of the area consists of trees such as acacia, herbs, grasses, kiwano melon, African horned cucumber, jelly melon.

The fauna of the area consists of migratory birds, snakes, insects, elephants, giraffes,

---

HINT

Don't confuse a dash with a hyphen (-) or an underscore (_) on your keyboard. We often use hyphens to make compound words.
A dash can be an effective device to use in your writing but you should not over-use it.

EXERCISE 1.3

1   Rewrite these sentences using dashes where appropriate to give emphasis or to show a range of numbers.

a   Ranked world number one by the Women's Tennis Association (WTA) eight times. She is considered one of the greatest champions ever.

b   It can get very hot in summer, more than 30 °C.

c   Temperatures range between 21 and 25 °C in spring.

d   I really like this apartment. Lots of potential!

HINT

Use key words to list key information. For example:
Area: about 900,000 square kilometres

Reading and speaking

A bus timetable

Activity 1.6

In a small group, discuss the information in the timetable below.
1 What is the purpose of this text?
2 How is the information presented? What do you need to read first in order to understand it?

Extract: City Safari

Penrose City Attractions offers a bus shuttle service to and from the city.

From City

Time			Location	Pick-Up Point
6.00 p.m.	7.00 p.m.	8.00 p.m.	Lakeside Hotel	Bus stop outside park (north gate)
6.03 p.m.	7.03 p.m.	8.03 p.m.	Yates Heights	Bus stop outside shopping mall
6.05 p.m.	7.05 p.m.	8.05 p.m.	Park View Hotel	Outside hotel lobby
6.10 p.m.	7.10 p.m.	8.10 p.m.	Penrose Plaza	Bus stop on south of plaza
6.12 p.m.	7.12 p.m.	8.12 p.m.	Luxe Aparthotel	Bus stop opposite hotel
6.15 p.m.	7.15 p.m.	8.15 p.m.	Central Hotel	Taxi stand at Gosport Lane
6.20 p.m.	7.20 p.m.	8.20 p.m.	City Hotel	Bus stop opposite hotel on Waldorf St
6.25 p.m.	7.25 p.m.	8.25 p.m.	William Road (near fountain)	Bus stop outside Jones store (west entrance)
6.30 p.m.	7.30 p.m.	8.30 p.m.	Canada Hotel	Outside hotel lobby
7.00 p.m.	8.00 p.m.	9.00 p.m.	City Safari	

To City

Time	Location	Pick-Up Point
Every half hour, from 9.00 p.m. to 11.30 p.m.	City Safari	At the bus stop outside the City Safari

Fare Type	Adult	Child
Single Trip	$4.00/trip	$2.00/trip
Daily Pass	$12.00/day (24hrs)	$6.00/day (24hrs)

Spotlight on: layout
Some information is best presented in a table or a diagram. This makes it quick and easy to read.

EXERCISE 1.4

Work in a pair. Ask and answer questions about the timetable. Here are some examples to get you started.
- How much would it cost you to travel from the City Safari to Penrose City and back again?
- Where would you have to go to meet the bus if you were staying at the Canada Hotel and how long would it take to get to the zoo?

Spotlight on: informative descriptions

Informative descriptions give readers facts, descriptions and illustrations or diagrams to help them to understand information.

Reading

Writing with factual descriptions

Activity 1.7

1. Work in a pair. Skim the text quickly, reading the headings and the captions under the photographs. Discuss briefly what the text is about.
2. Take turns to read the text aloud to each other, paragraph by paragraph. Identify what you think are the main ideas.

HINT

You do not have to understand every word in the text to get the **gist** (main idea) of the meaning. Focus on getting the gist first, then go back and read again in more detail.

EXERCISE 1.5

Read this text silently to yourself. As you read, write down what you think are the key words. For example: *Pompeii (Roman city), Mount Vesuvius, volcano, eruption.*

Extract: Pompeii

In the first century CE, Pompeii was a large and busy Roman city on the Bay of Naples in the Mediterranean. It was destroyed when the volcano named Mount Vesuvius erupted. Many of the inhabitants of the city were killed as a result of the eruption but the city remained covered in volcanic ash, leaving behind a perfectly preserved example of city life in Roman times. The eruption of Mount Vesuvius that took place on 24 August 79CE

Pompeii as it looks today

destroyed not only Pompeii but also nearby cities such as Herculaneum. Like Pompeii, Herculaneum was entirely covered by the volcanic ash and hot mud which Vesuvius belched forth. It was only 1600 years after the eruption that these cities were rediscovered when archaeologists began to excavate the sites. Many of the buildings and streets have now been revealed and large numbers of artefacts giving evidence of the everyday life of the ancient inhabitants have been discovered, but the process of excavation continues. There are still many areas to excavate and explore.

What was Pompeii like before the explosion?

Pompeii had a population of about 20 000 people and it was a sophisticated city: houses had indoor running water and there was a lively marketplace, an amphitheatre for different types of entertainment and a well-organised local government. There were many wealthy people living there as we can deduce from the beautiful works of art found

▲ This is a street food shop in Pompeii

in many of the houses. As in other Roman cities, there were public baths, cobbled streets, sidewalks and a large number of shops selling everything the population would require.

◄ Ancient graffiti in Latin on the street walls

What happened when the volcano exploded?

Before the actual eruption, there had been rumblings coming from Vesuvius (which is not uncommon in volcanic areas) and people recorded seeing a very large cloud resting above the mountain. We now know that this was a cloud of volcanic ash and cinders, but at the time people thought this cloud was harmless. Volcanic ash, however, is thick, heavy and falls in huge amounts, accompanied by hot cinders and rocks; it chokes and suffocates all breathing beings and this is what happened to so many of the residents of Pompeii and Herculaneum. Pompeii and Herculaneum were buried beneath 3 metres of ash and debris. Few people managed to escape.

We know what happened when Vesuvius erupted because a Roman official and writer called Pliny the Younger witnessed it and he described what he saw to his friend, who was the historian Tacitus. He also helped to rescue some people there.

▲ An ash and rock volcanic eruption like the one that destroyed Pompeii

HINT

Make sure that your handwriting is clear even though you are writing fast or making rough notes!

EXERCISE 1.6

1   Refer to the list of key words that you made. Make short notes from the text, using bullet points, of all the factual details about Pompeii and the people who lived there before the eruption of Mount Vesuvius in 79CE.

2   Now write a second group of notes containing all the facts about the eruption of Mount Vesuvius and its effects on the surrounding area.

EXTENSION

Work in a small group. Compare the notes you have written for questions 1 and 2 with the original article.
- What parts of the original article have not been included in your note versions of the events?
- Do you think that these 'missing' parts help to make the communication of the facts more interesting to a reader? Give reasons for your answer.

Key skills

Word families

Words in a word family have the same main part or root. For example, the words *erupt*, *eruption*, *erupted* and *erupting* all belong to the same word family.

We add prefixes or suffixes to a root to add meaning to the words. For example:

- Add **-ing** or **-e**d to show verb tenses like the present continuous or a past tense.
- Form different parts of speech like **nouns**, **adjectives** and **adverbs** by adding suffixes such as **-able**, **-ness**, **-ish** or **-ly**.
- Make words with opposite meanings by using prefixes such as **non-** and **un-**.
- Make comparative adjectives and adverbs by adding **-er** and **-est**.

Why is this important?

If you know what *erupt* means, you can work out what the other words in the family mean.

If you know how to spell *erupt* and the suffix *-ion*, you can work out how to spell *eruption*.

> **EXERCISE 1.7**
>
> Use your knowledge of word families to write the words in brackets in the correct forms.
>
> **Other disasters also struck Pompeii**
>
> There have been other natural disasters that (affect) Pompeii. In 62CE, only 17 years before the (erupt), the city had to be (build) after (suffer) an earthquake.
>
> In the year 202CE, Vesuvius (erupt) again and this time the (erupt) lasted for a whole week. There was another major eruption in 1631CE, which killed about 3000 people, and there were further eruptions in 1631, 1913 and most (recent) in 1944. Vesuvius remains an active and (potential) (danger) volcano.

Activity 1.8

Read the following informative description in a pair.

1 Use your knowledge of word families to work out the meanings of the words in bold.

2 Say if each word is a noun, an adjective, an adverb or a verb. If the word is a verb, say what tense it is in.

Herculaneum was an ancient town, **located** in Campania, Italy. The city was **destroyed** and buried under **volcanic** ash and pumice in the eruption of Mount Vesuvius in 79CE. The city was **blanketed** in thick ash which **preserved** it and protected it against looting. **Excavations** have revealed a town with many **luxurious** villas, **characteristic** of a wealthy population. Only part of the city has been excavated, and much attention is given to the **preservation** of the excavated parts. Rules for visiting the site are strictly **enforced**.

> **KEY WORDS**
>
> **noun** a word that gives the name of a person, place, thing or abstract idea
>
> **adjective** a word that describes a noun
>
> **adverb** a word that gives more information about an action or an adjective

Spotlight on: instructional texts

Instructional texts explain how to make or do things. They use layout features such as numbering or bullet points to organise information.

Activity 1.9

Read the following recipe in a pair.

1 Explain briefly to your partner how to make chocolate brownies.

2 Make your own notes about the features of recipe texts, for example, layout, vocabulary, punctuation and illustration.

Reading and speaking

LET'S TALK

What is your favourite meal? Find a recipe for the meal in a recipe book or online and bring a copy to your group. Discuss the recipes: comment on the layout of the recipe (how the information is organised).

- Which one is easiest to read? Why?
- What type of punctuation is used in each recipe? How does this help us read the information?
- Look at the instructions. Which verbs are commonly used? What form are they in?

A recipe

Extract: Chocolate brownies

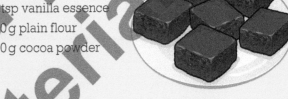

Makes 6 large pieces

Ingredients:

200 g dark chocolate
100 g unsalted butter, softened
250 g caster sugar
4 eggs, beaten

1 tsp vanilla essence
60 g plain flour
60 g cocoa powder

Directions:

1 Preheat the oven to 165 °C and grease and line a 15 cm by 15 cm square brownie tin or baking tin.

2 Break up the chocolate into small pieces in a heatproof bowl and melt it down over a pan of gently simmering water. Remove from the heat and leave to cool until needed.

3 Whisk the butter and sugar together until they are light and fluffy and then gradually beat in the eggs. Add the vanilla essence and mix well.

4 Fold in the melted chocolate mixture and then sift in the flour and cocoa.

5 When the mixture is well combined, transfer to the prepared tin and cook for 25 to 30 minutes until cooked – the brownies should still be soft in the middle.

6 Transfer to a wire rack to cool and then cut into pieces.

HINT

You need to think about layout, punctuation and sentence structures. Pay attention to the order (sequence) of instructions and make sure the instructions are clear.

EXERCISE 1. 8

Rewrite the following recipe in a way that makes it clear and easy to follow.

How to make a healthy toastie

Toasties are delicious and can be quite healthy too. All you need is some good bread, cheese and then perhaps some pickles, tomatoes or other veggies. They only take a few minutes and you can make them in a special machine or in a frying pan. Slice the bread and cheese – add some butter if you like. Piling the ingredients between the slices of bread is the fun bit! Then you can enjoy. Cooking should take about 5 minutes – until brown and gooey!

Spotlight on: information texts that entertain

Some texts can entertain while providing information. Think about the advice columns online or in magazines, for example.

Activity 1.10

1 Read the following extract, which explains the rules of cricket. Try reading it aloud with a partner.

2 Did you understand or were you confused? If you know the rules of cricket, can you explain them to your partner in a different way? Look for some help online if you are not sure.

HINT
Try to read ahead as you read aloud. This can help you understand what you are reading.

Information that entertains

EXERCISE 1.9

Bill is an agony uncle. This is somebody who gives personal advice to readers in a magazine, newspaper or online.

Read the following letter to the column and Bill's reply, then answer the questions.

1 What is the purpose of this text?

2 Who is the audience (who is it written for)?

3 What information does Bill give in the reply?

4 Do you think this reply is helpful or not? Give a reason for your answer.

5 Write your own answer to this letter.

Extract: Advice column

Dear Bill

I need some advice. It's about my dad. He just loves to play a game that he says is called Pokémon GO. It's so embarrassing to go out with him. He's always looking at his phone and chasing things around. I'm worried he is going to knock someone over! What is this game and what should I do?

Deirdre

Dear Deidre

My advice to you is to download the game and play it with your dad. It's fun – I have played it myself! Then you can also help your dad to stay safe. Bumping into others while you play can be a problem. You can find out more about the game and how to play it online.

Uncle Bill

Extract: The rules of cricket

- You have two sides, one out in the field and one in.
- When you are in the side that's in, you stay in until you are out and then the next player comes in.
- When you are all out, the side that's out comes in and the side that's been in goes out and tries to get those coming in out.
- Sometimes there are players still in and not out.
- When both sides have been in and all the players are out (including those who are not out), then the game is finished.

Key skills

Bias

If you show bias, it means you show prejudice against a thing, a person or a group of people in a way that is not fair. For example:

- **Racism** is bias against people of other racial groups.
- **Sexism** is bias against people of different genders.
- **Ageism** is bias against older or younger people.

Writers can introduce bias in information texts by voicing opinions rather than only giving factual information.

A writer's choice of words can be biased. For example, if a writer says that 'this place is only for old people' it shows bias against young people (because they're not welcome in that place) and bias towards old people (because they are more welcome in that place).

The use of punctuation can also introduce bias. Remember that dashes can emphasise certain words, for example.

Read the information about bias and make sure you understand what it is, then read this article from a school newspaper.

Extract: An article in a school newspaper

by Kim Taehyung

Why go to a zoo in the day – when you can visit one by night? The City Safari is a top attraction in Penrose City. It is a nocturnal zoo – a zoo where animals sleep by day and come out at night!

The City Safari attracts about 1.1 million visitors a year. It has over 700 animals and over 100 specials. Of those, about 38% are threatened species. The animals are not kept in cages but are separated from visitors by natural barriers. Girls – do not visit the snake or scorpion exhibit – it is way too scary for you!

No animal is as impressive as the tiger – and the City Safari even has an **ambush** of white Bengal tigers! There are many walking trails to explore all areas of the park. Do not worry, older people – you can also explore the park by tram.

GLOSSARY
ambush the name for a group of tigers

Activity 1.11

Work in a small group and discuss these questions.

1 How has the author shown bias in the text above? Toward which group(s) has the author shown bias?

2 How could you remove the bias from the text? Think bout the choice of words and the punctuation.

3 In what other texts are we likely to find bias? How we avoid bias?

Speaking and listening

Giving clear information

Study the map of the City Safari on page 15.

Spotlight on: working in groups

Take turns and different roles in the group as necessary. Be sensitive to other speakers.
Do not speak when someone else is speaking.

Activity 1.12

Give your classmate directions about getting to a specific part of the zoo.

Remember that you should use appropriate non-verbal techniques (such as hand gestures) to help convey meaning.

EXERCISE 1.10

Prepare a talk about the features of the City Safari.

■ When giving a talk or making a speech, you may use notes as aids but try not to read directly from them. Use dashes in your notes to remind yourself about where to pause and what to emphasise.

■ Speak clearly and adjust your pace and **tone** to make yourself understood. Add interesting factual information and exciting descriptions to make your talk interesting to the listeners.

■ At the end of any spoken presentation, take some time to evaluate how well it went and to identify ways in which it could have been improved.

Activity 1.13

In a small group, discuss the map on page 15.

1 Is a visual text also a text? Why?
2 What is the purpose of this map?
3 What text features does the visual text show?
4 Is this visual text better to communicate information about the zoo? Why?
5 What are the visual text's limitations?
6 What improvements could you make to this visual text to make it more user-friendly?

Legend

- Toilet
- Restaurant
- Shelter
- Bus stop
- Bus route
- Walking route
- Accessible route
- Savannah Street
- Monkey Magic
- Tiger Trail
- Wildebeest Walk

Activity 1.14

In a small group, discuss the map on page 15.

1 Is a visual text also a text? Why?
2 What is the purpose of this map?
3 What text features does the visual text show?
4 Is this visual text better to communicate information about the zoo? Why?
5 What are the visual text's limitations?
6 What improvements could you make to this visual text to make it more user-friendly?

KEY WORD

tone what the author feels or wants the reader to feel about something. Tone can be humorous, dark or angry, for example

Extract: A visual text

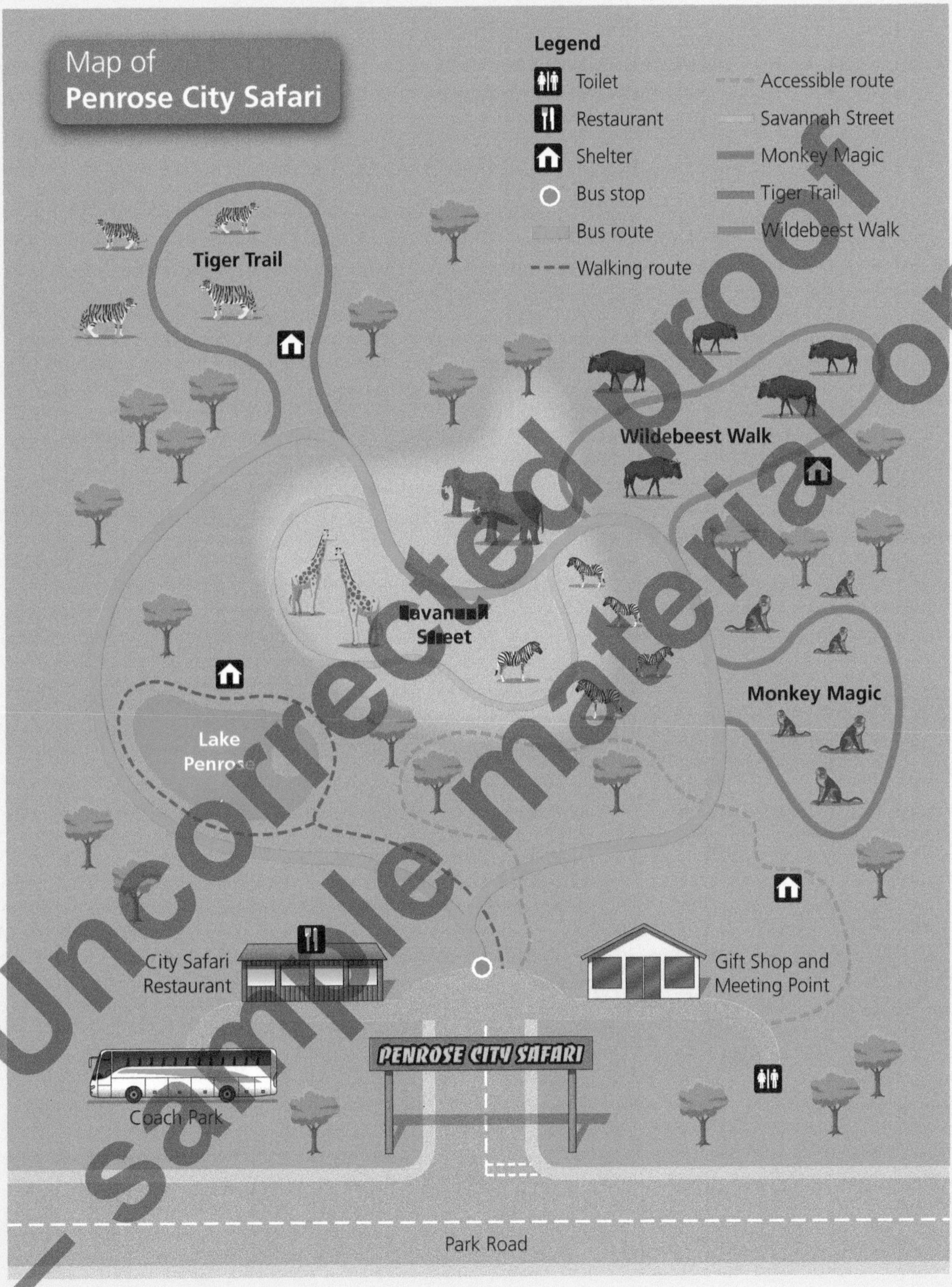

Map of Penrose City Safari

Legend

🚻 Toilet		┄┄	Accessible route
🍴 Restaurant		──	Savannah Street
🏠 Shelter		──	Monkey Magic
○ Bus stop		──	Tiger Trail
Bus route		──	Wildebeest Walk
┄┄ Walking route			

Tiger Trail

Wildebeest Walk

Savannah Street

Monkey Magic

Lake Penrose

City Safari Restaurant

Gift Shop and Meeting Point

PENROSE CITY SAFARI

Coach Park

Park Road

Key skills

Revise paragraphs and topic sentences

Good writers organise their ideas clearly when they write. They list their main ideas, divide their writing into paragraphs and make sure that each paragraph contains only one main topic or idea. The other sentences in the paragraph are there to support the main idea.

A **paragraph** is a group of closely related sentences that develop a central idea. Writers give structure and organisation to their work by dividing a piece of continuous writing into paragraphs. When you are planning your own writing, it helps to plan your work by thinking about paragraphs and their topics. Look at this paragraph about the volcano that destroyed Pompeii.

All paragraphs should contain a **topic sentence**. It contains the main point of the paragraph.

What happened when the volcano exploded?

Vesuvius is a composite volcano. Volcanoes of this type have two different types of eruptions: one type is like the spectacular eruptions depicted in disaster films in which the volcano blasts out torrents of molten lava; the other type is where the volcano blows out ash and rock. The eruption that destroyed Pompeii and Herculaneum was of the second type.

The rest of the paragraph should relate to the topic sentence in a logical and **coherent** way.

KEY WORDS

topic sentence a sentence that contains the main topic or summary of the paragraph. It is usually the first sentence in a paragraph
coherent in a way that makes sense; is clear and well-planned

EXERCISE 1.11

Write one paragraph of informative text about a place that you know well or have visited. Write the topic sentence first. This sentence should tell the reader what the place is and where it is. Then write 4–5 supporting sentences to give a fuller description of the place.

EXTENSION

Update the paragraph on Serena Williams (page 4) to the present time. Separate it into a few logical paragraphs. Remember to write a great topic sentence for each paragraph.

Writing

Information texts

EXERCISE 1.12

Write instructions about how to make a box kite. Look at the pictures below. Think about what materials you might need to do this and how you could make the kite. Make some rough notes and do some online research if necessary before you begin.

1. Use the relevant text features for this type of writing. Think about the features you will use.
2. Plan your writing. Use a mind-map to organise your ideas.
3. When you have completed writing your instructions, ask your partner to read and edit them to improve your language, grammar and the structure of your text.

> **HINT**
> Think about the text features that were used in the recipe you read. Numbering, bullets and headings would be useful here. Keep the instructions as simple as possible! Think about the text features that were used in the recipe you read. Numbering, bullets and headings would be useful here. Keep the instructions as simple as possible!

Activity 1.15

Work in a small group. You are going to plan and write a two-page information brochure for a tourist attraction such as a theme park or a nature reserve with animals.

1. Choose your topic and plan your brochure. Think about all the information that you want to provide. The information must be factual and useful. Use a spider diagram or mind-map to do your planning and organise your ideas. You can also use a rough piece of paper to plan the layout of the brochure. Decide which illustrations you will need and where you will place them.
2. Do your research and draft the text. Remember to use bullets and punctuation such as dashes and brackets to make the text easy to read. Each person in the group should make a contribution and write one short paragraph of information with a good topic sentence.
3. Edit and improve your brochure. You can choose to produce the final brochure by hand or you can use a computer.
4. Present your brochure to the class.

SELF-CHECK

- ☐ Is your layout clear and easy to read?
- ☐ Is your spelling correct? Use your knowledge of word families.
- ☐ Is the information accurate and interesting?
- ☐ Have you used punctuation to make the text clear?
- ☐ Have you included photographs or illustrations (or perhaps a map if that is useful?)

> **HINT**
> Use The Writing Cycle on page v for further help.

Reviewing

Reflect on the non-fiction texts you've read in this chapter

Talk about:

- which texts you liked and which you didn't like
- which you think were well-written and why
- what techniques the writers used to create effects in their writing
- what texts you have read that are similar to these.

Activity 1.16

Look back at the extracts from pages 2–12. Work in a group to evaluate their purpose and their effectiveness. Match the text types to their definitions:

Text types	Definitions
advice columns	to give visitors ideas of where to go and what to do in a specific country or place
recipes	to give people help and guidance on a particular issue
online encyclopedias	a table or chart showing the departure and arrival times of transport, e.g. buses
visual texts	a text giving in-depth information on a specific subject
timetables	a list of instructions and ingredients needed to make a certain type of food
advertisements	a text to show how something works or the layout of an area
tourist guides	a short text or visual to promote or publicise a product

Try to find your own examples of each type of text. How often do you use each text type?

If you like reading non-fiction, try these books:

- *Some Writer! The Story of E.B. White* by Melissa Sweet
- *What Color Is My World? The Lost History of African-American Inventors* by Kareem Abdul-Jabbar and Raymond Obstfeld
- *Women in Science: 50 Fearless Pioneers Who Changed the World* by Rachel Ignotofsky
  Totally Wacky Facts About History by Cari Meister

Reflect on your learning in this chapter

- What techniques have you learned to improve your reading, listening and speaking and writing?
- Make a list of the things you would like to practise further.
  - Compile a plan for tackling these.
  - Discuss your lists and ideas with your classmates and your teacher.

2 When I was young ...

Reading
★ Autobiographical texts
★ Poems about childhood and school
★ Building up detail

Speaking and listening
★ Formal and informal register
★ Listening to real-life characters
★ A reading of an autobiographical piece

WHEN I WAS YOUNG...

Writing
★ Planning and drafting personal writing
★ autobiographical piece for performance

Key skills
★ Distinctive voices
★ Adverbs in dialogues
★ Writing in dialogue

LET'S TALK
Autobiographies are true stories about people's lives, told by the people themselves. (Biographies are told by another person such as a journalist.)

- What famous biographies or autobiographies do you know? Which have you read?
- Why do you think they were written?
- What are the features of a good autobiography?

- How are autobiographies different from other non-fiction texts?
- How are autobiographies similar to fiction genres such as short stories or novels?

Reading

A writer's choices

These are sentences from different **autobiographies**.

When I was born, people in our village commiserated with my mother and nobody congratulated my father.

When the race began I tried not to rationalize or demand too much logic from what was taking place. But it was madness to the nth degree.

It was a very little shop, in a shabby block of other small shops and offices. Its window, however, sparkled with polishing despite the overcast day.

If I left the house with a clean uniform, it was guaranteed to come home dirty.

Activity 2.1

Work with a partner. Take it in turns to read the extracts to each other.

1   Each of these sentences is a tiny story on its own. Discuss each sentence with a partner. Make some guesses or predictions using these questions:

■   What details are we given? What other details can we guess?
■   What could be the background to this?
■   Where do you expect the writer to take you next?
■   What questions would you ask the author, to gain more information?

In each sentence, the writer has chosen to link ideas by using these words: *when, if, but, whenever.*

a   Find these words in the extracts.
b   Discuss what you know about how these words work to connect sentences.
c   Discuss how these have been used to engage you as a reader.

3   The writers have used these words to create mini-surprises in their sentences.

   Choose one sentence to write about.
   Explain what the surprise is, and how it might grab the reader's curiosity. Give a full response.

4   These sentences are from four different autobiographies.

■   From the small extracts, which would you be most interested in reading? Why?
■   Does it fit in with what you normally enjoy reading?
■   Share your personal choices and reasons with your partner, or with a small group.

Building up detail

Author: Steven Gerrard

Steven Gerrard (born in 1980) is the manager of Scottish club Rangers. He was one of the best footballers in the world, captaining both Liverpool and England and retired in 2016.

> If I left the house with a clean uniform, it was guaranteed to come home dirty. The same with shoes. Scuffed and muddy. Every time. Mum went up the wall.

> When I was naughty, the teachers made me stand by the wall, looking at the bricks for five minutes as punishment. I never bullied anyone. I never hurt anyone or swore. I was just cheeky and mischievous. My crimes were petty ones: answering back or going on muddy grass when we were told to stay on the yard. Usual kids' stuff.

> Still now I hate Sunday nights. Still!

> Steam almost rose from my pencil I wrote so furiously. The teachers must have thought I was focusing really hard on the lesson. I'm sorry. I wasn't.
>
> Steven Gerrard

EXERCISE 2.1

Write a short character description of Steven Gerrard as a young child at school. Use evidence from the extracts to support your interpretation.

KEY WORD

rhythm the pattern of beats in a poem or a sentence

Key skills

Distinctive voices

In the extracts above, the author mixes longer sentences with very short, simple sentences or phrases to finish a thought. This is a useful technique to portray the voice and personality of the author.

Activity 2.3

Find examples of these short, punchy sentences and phrases in the extracts.

Re-read each extract out loud. Try to put some of the personality of the young child into your reading. Work together to decide on the tone of voice to use, the **rhythm** of speech, and the gestures you could make to bring the voice of this young child to life. Use the mixture of long and short, simple sentences to help you perform the work.

Activity 2.2

These extracts are taken from the part of the book that describes Steven Gerrard's early memories of school.

Work with a partner. Take it in turns to read the extracts to each other then discuss these questions.

1 What is Gerrard's personality like?

2 Are there any phrases that confuse you? What could 'Mum went up the wall' mean?

3 What do you notice about the lengths of the sentences?

Writing

Planning and drafting personal writing

You are going to develop a piece of personal writing to narrate an event or memory from your early school days.

Activity 2.4

To generate some ideas, work in a small group.

Take it in turns to describe your memories of your first day of school.

Use these questions to prompt your answers.

> What was the classroom like? What about the playground?

> What did you have for lunch?

> What other details do you remember vividly?

Try to be as specific as possible. Here are some further questions to ask:
- Who was there?
- Who was your teacher? Do you remember what they looked like? Did they seem friendly or stern?
- Did you know anyone already, or did you have to make new friends?

Now take a moment to reflect on how it felt to be there on your first day. Choose words from this list that describe how you felt:
- joyful
- afraid
- confident
- shy
- excited
- anxious
- lonely
- overwhelmed
- important
- unimportant

Reflection and note-taking

When you have listened to everyone in your group and helped bring their memories to life, spend some time writing notes about your own memories.

Write down some sentences that occur to you now, to describe the classroom, the teacher and other pupils, and how you felt on the day. Don't try to write a full paragraph or extract: just write your ideas in sentences.

This is one useful planning method. Some of these sentences will be useful when you write more fully later.

Organise and shape your ideas

You have started to plan some writing by talking in a group, answering questions, and then writing down sentence notes. Now it is time to develop your writing more fully.

Shape your ideas

Remember – specific details paint a more vivid picture than vague statements.

Compare these sentences:
I was shy.
I hid behind my mum's legs.

The specific details of a child trying to hide brings the shyness to life.

Go through your notes. Pick one or two sentences to shape by making them more specific. Describe concrete details and behaviours, rather than vague feelings.

Organise your ideas

Your notes are not connected yet.

Think about how your experiences of that day are connected. You could arrange your ideas in time sequence:
When I arrived, …
The first thing I noticed …
After I'd built up courage …
The next thing I knew …

You could storyboard your ideas to help plan the sequence

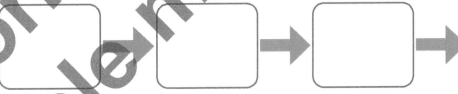

Develop a viewpoint

Remember how Steven Gerrard brought the sense of being a young child to life? He mixed some longer thoughts with the shorter reaction sentences and statements. Think about how you will build detail and feelings into your sentences. What personality will you try to show?

Write!

Use the notes and your planning ideas to generate a short passage to describe your early memories of school.

Your goals are:
- to describe the memory with specific details
- to organise the ideas so a reader can follow what is going on
- to express the viewpoint of that young child (you!).

The Great Depression was a huge global economic downturn in the 1930s, which began in the USA and lasted almost a decade.

How does the time setting play a part in the central theme of the story? What do we learn about what it was like growing up in an industrial city during this time?

Listening

Real-life characters

In this extract, the author describes an episode involving her mother. Listen to the full extract and notice how the author brings two characters to life.

Author: Helen Forrester

Helen Forrester (1919-2011) was the pen name of June Bhatia. She wrote books about her early childhood in Liverpool during the Great Depression, including *Liverpool Miss*, as well as several works of fiction.

Extract: *Liverpool Miss*

It was a very little shop, in a shabby block of other small shops and offices. Its window, however, sparkled with polishing despite the overcast day. Through the gleaming glass I could dimly see rows of large bottles of sweets and in front of them an arrangement of chocolate boxes, all of them free of dust. Beneath the window, a sign in faded gold lettering advertised Fry's Chocolate.

Mother, who had not spoken to me during the walk, paused in front of the shop and frowned. Then she swung open the glass-paned door and stalked in. I followed her, my heart going pit-a-pat, in unison with the click of Mother's shoes on the highly polished, though worn, linoleum within.

An old-fashioned bell hung on a spring attached to the door was still tinkling softly when a stout, middle-aged woman with a beaming smile on her round face emerged through a lace-draped door leading to an inner room.

'Yes, luv?' she inquired cheerfully.

'I understand that you wrote to my daughter about a post in your shop?' Mother's voice was perfectly civil, but the word 'post' instead of 'job' sounded sarcastic.

The smile was swept from the woman's face. She looked us both up and down uncertainly, while I agonised over what Mother might say next.

'Helen?' the woman asked, running a stubby finger along her lower lip.

'Helen Forrester,' replied Mother icily.

Helen Forrester

Activity 2.5

1 Summarise the event described, using a table like this:

Setting	
Characters	
Main event	

2 Compare and contrast the personalities of the mother and the shop owner.
3 Listen again to the extract. Take notes of words or phrases that tell you something about the personality of each person.
4 Write a character description of each person, using evidence from your notes to support your ideas
   The author writes that …
   … which shows that …
   I interpreted this word to mean …

Key skills

Adverbs in dialogue

The author uses dialogue to help describe the scene and show the two personalities.

Look at these examples:
   'Yes, luv?' she inquired **cheerfully**.
   'Helen Forrester,' replied Mother **icily**.

The author has used adverbs to indicate how the speech has been said. Use these adverbs and work together to say the dialogue out loud. Perform the speech in the way the adverb tells you.

Now try switching the adverbs:
   'Yes, luv?' she inquired **icily**.
   'Helen Forrester,' replied Mother **cheerfully**.

Substitute different adverbs from below and perform the dialogue to match the new adverbs.

seriously	hopefully	confidently
furiously	desperately	shyly
confusedly	fearfully	cautiously

With this simple technique, an author can adapt dialogue to show different feelings and personalities.

Now listen to this extract. Amryl Johnson revisits the Caribbean island of Tobago where she lived as a child. She describes an event that she witnessed during her visit.

Author: Amryl Johnson

Amryl Johnson (1944-2001) was born in Tunapuna, Trinidad, but moved to Britain when she was 11. She taught at the University of Warwick and wrote poems, short stories and novels.

Activity 2.6

1   Summarise the event described, using the same type of table as before.

Setting	
Characters	
Main event	

'The crab dead! All you can't see the crab dead?!!'

I felt the protestors had a point. The only movement from the crab was an involuntary one made by any motion of the string.

'How all you people so blasted stupid? All you can't see the crab already dead when he haul it across the line?!'

This was very interesting. The crab went into a series of jerks as the minder worked the string to demonstrate it was still in the land of the living. Alternatively, it could indeed have been involuntary. Death throes.

'How man in he right mind go want pin medal on dead crab?!'

Amryl Johnson

The author presents the dialogue as spoken by people in the scene, but does not name each speaker. Instead, the jumble of voices is part of the scene, telling the story.

The dialogue is written as non-standard English.
Why do you think the author chose to use this technique?
How can you tell the dialogue is non-standard English?
How does this help bring the scene to life?
Rewrite lines of dialogue in standard English. Try reading them out loud with a partner, and compare with the originals. Think about the different effects.

KEY WORDS

Speech marks (' ') or **inverted commas** punctuation marks used to indicate the beginning and end of direct speech. They can also be used for quotations and titles

direct speech the words actually spoken by someone, indicated by speech marks

phrase a group of words with no verb

Activity 2.7

Copy these sentences, adding the correct punctuation.

1 Have you ever worked before she asked me

2 She asked me have you ever worked before

3 I have worked but only at home I replied

4 I replied I have worked but only at home

5 What work would Helen be expected to do asked Mother

6 Mother asked what work would Helen be expected to do

7 Well now I hadn't exactly thought of anything she said

8 She said well now I hadn't exactly thought of anything

Key skills

Writing dialogue

We have looked at how authors have used dialogue to bring their personal memories to life for a reader.

Now it is your turn to add some dialogue to your writing.

First, let's revise some key skills.

Punctuating statements and questions in dialogue

If a person has made a statement, then a comma comes before the **speech marks** in **direct speech**.

> 'Helen Forrester,' replied Mother icily.

If a person asks a question, the question mark comes before the speech marks.

> 'Yes, luv?' she inquired cheerfully.

You can also write the speech at the end of a sentence, using a comma before the speech marks begin.

> I nodded negatively. Then cleared my throat and said, 'Only at home.'

Direct and reported speech

You can also report speech indirectly.

Look at these examples.

Direct speech	Indirect speech
'The crab dead!' one man shouted.	One man shouted that the crab was dead.
'It dead before it cross the line!' a spectator announced.	A spectator announced that the crab had been dead before it crossed the line.
'I see he move!' a little boy said in excitement.	In excitement, a little boy said that he saw the crab move.

You can write indirect speech by starting with a **phrase** like this:

> He said that …   She asked if …   I agreed that …

Remember – you don't write the exact words, but report the meaning of what they said.

EXERCISE 2.2

Rewrite these sentences as indirect speech.

1 'Can't you see the crab dead?' he asked.

2 'You're a cheat!' she said.

3 'He the winner,' I announced.

Add dialogue for a purpose

You can use dialogue to:
- show personality or feelings
- bring a scene to life
- move the story along.

LET'S TALK

Go back to your writing about early school memories.

Work with a partner. Share your writing and talk about where you could each add dialogue for a purpose.

- Could you use dialogue to show the personality of a teacher, parent or other pupil?
- What part of the story could you tell through dialogue?
- Would you use standard or non-standard English?

Help each other to decide where and how to add dialogue.

HINT

Remember how Helen Forrester used the adverbs 'icily' and 'cheerfully' in her dialogue to help show character and feelings? Choose some adverbs to add to some of the dialogue you use.

nervously	timidly	threateningly
tearfully	angrily	gravely
fiercely	hopefully	sternly

Use a dictionary or thesaurus to help choose the appropriate adverbs for your dialogue.

Activity 2.8

Now write the scene, including three or four lines of dialogue.
You can use a mixture of direct and indirect speech.
Your goal is to use dialogue to bring the characters and feelings to life.
When you have completed your writing, swap your work with a partner, and act as critical friends.
  Check for accurate punctuation.
  Check for adverbs.
  Check for how the dialogue helps bring the feelings to life.
Share some positive praise and some comments for how to improve.

Author: Malala Yousafzai

Malala Yousafzai was shot by the Taliban (an Islamic political movement and military organisation based in Afghanistan) in 2012 because she demanded that girls should get an education. She survived and, in 2014, she became the youngest person to receive the Nobel Peace Prize. She continues to fight for girls' education.

Spotlight on: political context

Political context is the setting of the story in a particular country's history. The way the country is governed, its laws and the way people are treated is thus central to the text.

LONG PAGE

Reading

Activity 2.9

Think about these questions and discuss them in a small group.
1   Have you heard of Malala before?
2   Do you know anything about the Nobel Peace Prize?
3   What political background is she writing in?
4   What issues are important to her?
5   Do you have any strong beliefs about education?

Activity 1.10

'I arrived at dawn as the last star blinked out.'
This is the second sentence of the extract. Before you read on, discuss what you think it could mean. Guess the importance of this image.
Discuss your predictions as a class.

Activity 1.11

Use the history of these words (their etymology) to work out their meaning:
- commiserated – 'com' (from Latin meaning 'with') and 'miserari' (to cry or feel miserable)
- auspicious – from the Latin 'avis' (bird) and 'specere' (to look at): looking at birds to foretell the future
Find these words in the text. Does your predicted meaning make sense?

Now read this extract from the autobiography of Malala Yousafzai.

Extract: *I Am Malala*

A daughter is born

WHEN I WAS born, people in our village **commiserated** with my mother and nobody congratulated my father. I arrived at dawn as the last star blinked out. We Pashtuns see this as an **auspicious** sign. My father didn't have any money for the hospital or for a midwife so a neighbour helped at my birth. My parents' first child was stillborn but I popped out kicking and screaming. I was a girl in a land where rifles are fired in celebration of a son, while daughters are hidden away behind a curtain, their role in life simply to prepare food and give birth to children. For most Pashtuns it's a gloomy day when a daughter is born. My father's cousin Jehan Sher Khan Yousafzai was one of the few who came to celebrate my birth and even gave a handsome gift of money.

Activity 1.12

Write a short response to the text summing up your thoughts to these questions and add any other personal responses you may have:
- Why did nobody congratulate her father?
- How do you feel about the issues she and her family faced?
- What verbs did Malala use to describe herself as a baby? What does this suggest about her personality?

29

WORD ATTACK SKILLS

Part of this style is a use of rich vocabulary. Look for the following words in the text:
- ✔ vast
- ✔ astonishment
- ✔ roam
- ✔ tradition

Predict the meaning of each word, then define each word fully using a dictionary. Write the definitions of each word and look for synonyms. Save these words and synonyms to use in your own writing.

EXERCISE 2.3

Use evidence from the text to write a character description of Malala's father. Your goal is to show how you have understood the character of her father and his feelings towards the issues they faced.

The extract continues to give more information about Malala's childhood. Malala writes in a serious, formal tone to match the serious issues she and her family faced.

Yet, he brought with him a **vast** family tree of our clan, the Dalokhel Yousafzai, going right back to my great-great-grandfather and showing only the male line. My father, Ziauddin, is different from most Pashtun men. He took the tree, drew a line like a lollipop from his name and at the end of it he wrote, 'Malala'. His cousin laughed in **astonishment**. My father didn't care. He says he looked into my eyes after I was born and fell in love. He told people, 'I know there is something different about this child.' He even asked friends to throw dried fruits, sweets and coins into my cradle, something we usually only do for boys. I was named after Malalai of Maiwand, the greatest heroine of Afghanistan.

Near us on our street there was a family with a girl my age called Safina and two boys similar in age to my brothers, Babar and Basit. We all played cricket on the street or rooftops together, but I knew as we got older the girls would be expected to stay inside. We'd be expected to cook and serve our brothers and fathers. While boys and men could **roam** freely about town, my mother and I could not go out without a male relative to accompany us, even if it was a five-year-old boy! This was the **tradition**. I had decided very early I would not be like that. My father always said, 'Malala will be free as a bird.' But, as I watched my brothers running across the roof, flying their kites and skilfully flicking the strings back and forth to cut each other's down, I wondered how free a daughter could ever be.

Malala Yousafzai

Speaking and listening

Formal and informal register

We all use different registers when we speak to different people – we change the words and tone we use depending on the context, audience and purpose. Think about how you would address a teacher and how you speak to your friends, for example. You would probably adopt an **informal** register with your friends, where your language is likely to be conversational among a familiar audience. **Formal** registers are used for more professional contexts or when addressing people you don't know so well.

KEY WORDS

informal informal writing or speech takes a more casual, conversational or personal tone and may include slang or figures of speech and non-standard English

formal formal writing or speech uses a serious tone and is often used in professional settings and for letters, reports and academic essays. Standard punctuation and grammar are used and contractions are avoided

Activity 2.13

You have read some different extracts.

- Steven Gerrard used an informal tone to portray what it was like for him at school as a young boy. His sentences were often made of very short phrases, showing the energy and buzz of a young child.
- Amryl Johnson used non-standard English to represent local dialogue and the excitement of the event.
- Malala uses serious language to portray the serious issues of her childhood.

As a class, discuss when you change the tone of your speech or writing. Complete a table like this:

I use formal language when …	I use informal language when …

Now give examples of the kinds of vocabulary you would use in each situation.

Examples in a formal style	Examples in an informal style

Develop your use of formal and informal language

> **KEY WORD**
> **Script** the written text of a video, play, film or book

2.17

Activity 2.14

In a small group, choose one of following tasks, A or B, to role-play certain situations.

- Think about how your words and tone will change each time.
- Make sure that your body language mirrors your words and tone.

Task A

Using the Steven Gerrard extract, pretend that you are:

1. Steven Gerrard talking to one of your teachers when he catches you planning a football match instead of writing your English essay.
2. the headteacher speaking to Steven's mum about some of his behaviour.

Task B

Using the Malala Yousafzai extract, pretend that you are:

1. Malala's father speaking to his cousin to announce his daughter's birth.
2. Malala's father talking to a local government about his plans for a new school and the money he needs to build it.

You could write notes or a script to help you.

Your teacher will give you time to practise so that you can perform your role play for the class.

Using your skills

You have learned how to:

- vary your sentences to shape your ideas
- connect and order your sentences
- use dialogue to show personality and feelings
- choose vocabulary for formal or informal tones.

EXERCISE 2.4

Now it is time to practise your skills independently.

Choose a memorable event from your past to write about.
- It could be a funny or amusing episode.
- It could be about an event that involved overcoming worry or fear.
- It should be a strong memory for you that you want to bring to life for your readers.

Your goal is to use the skills you have developed in this chapter to:
- bring a memory to life
- choose a suitable tone and vocabulary
- use dialogue to show character and feelings
- build detail by varying your sentences.

Stage 1: Plan by making notes in sentence form, then ordering the events in a storyboard.

Stage 2: Write your extract, in one or two drafts.

You can organise your text into paragraphs, based on the order of events. Use connective phrases to help your reader understand the order of events and the causes:

"It began with..."

"Suddenly, ..."

"At that moment..."

"Shortly afterwards..."

Stage 3: Edit, checking you have met the goals of the task.

Speaking and listening

Give a spoken reading of your autobiographical piece

Now it is time to share your writing with the class. You will prepare and read your writing aloud.

Before you begin, agree a class or group set of ground rules for a positive atmosphere for speaking and listening.

Follow these prompts to help you in either the role of listener or performer.

Readers:

Read slowly and clearly.

Try to make some eye contact with your audience.

Match your tone of voice to the style and seriousness of your writing.

Use gestures to emphasise certain points.

Listeners:

The person speaking may feel embarrassed. Support them by listening openly.

Think sensitively about the speaker's feelings.

Save questions until the end.

If you have a question, make sure it is relevant before you ask.

Reading

Like authors, poets also use their own childhood memories for inspiration. On this page and the next page are two poems about childhood.

A poem about a child's future

> ### 'I Am A Child'
>
> I am a child,
> All the world waits for my coming,
> All the earth watches with interest
> To see what I shall become.
> The future hangs in the balance,
> For what I am
> The world of tomorrow will be.
>
> I am a child,
> I have come into your world
> About which I know nothing.
> Why I came I know not.
> How I came I know not.
> I am curious.
> I am interested.
>
> I am a child,
> You hold in your hand my destiny.
> You determine, largely,
> Whether I shall succeed or fail.
> Give me, I pray you,
> Those things that make for happiness.
> Train me, I beg you,
> That I may be a blessing to the world.
>
> Mamie Gene Cole
> This poem, written in Chinese and English, appears at the entrance to the Guideposts Kindergarten in Hong Kong.

WORD ATTACK SKILLS

Explain the meaning of the following words, as they are used in the poem.
- ✔ interest
- ✔ destiny
- ✔ blessing

KEY WORD

repetition to repeat words or phrases again and again

Spotlight on: audience

Who is the poet speaking to – the audience? How does this link to the purpose of the poem?

Look at all the **repetition** in the poem, for example, I am a child, I am, I know not, I pray you, I beg you. What is its effect?

Why does the poet use verbs that express the future?

Activity 2.15

1. Are there any special ideas that stand out for you in this poem? Why?
2. What do you understand by this line: 'The future hangs in the balance'?
3. The poet speaks of 'destiny'. What does this mean? Do you believe in a destiny? How does this concept relate to Malala's experience (see pages 28–29)?

A poem about school

Poet: Carol Ann Duffy

Carol Ann Duffy (born in 1955) is a British poet and playwright. From 2009 to 2019, she was Britain's poet laureate, so she composed poems for special occasions.

Spotlight on: theme
What is the central theme or idea of the poem? How does it link to the poem's purpose?

THINK ABOUT
When you call someone 'a star', what do you mean? What does Carol Ann Duffy mean?

KEY WORD
rhyme when the endings of two or more words sound alike, e.g. *lean* and *seen*

'Your School'

Your school knows the names of places –
Dhaka, Rajshahi, Sylket, Khulna, Chittagong
and where they are.
Your school knows where rivers rise –
the Ganges, Brahmaputra, Thames –
and knows which seas they join.

Your school knows the height of mountains
disappearing into cloud.
Your school knows important dates,
the days when history turned around
to stare the human race
straight in the face.

Your school knows the poets' names, long dead –
John Keats, Rabindranath Tagore, Sylvia Plath –
and what they said.
It knows the paintings hanging in the old gold frames
in huge museums
and how the artists lived and loved
who dipped their brushes in the vivid paint.

Your school knows the language of the world –
hello, namaskar, sat sri akal, as-salaam-o-aleykum, salut –
it knows the homes of faith,
the certainties of science,
the living art of sport.

Your school knows what Isaac Newton thought,
what William Shakespeare wrote
and what Mohammed taught.

Your school knows your name –
Shirin, Abdul, Aysha, Rayhan, Lauren, Jack –
and who you are.
Your school knows the most important thing to know
you are a star,
a star.

Carol Ann Duffy

Activity 2.16

1 Where is there **rhyme** in the poem? Why does the poet use it there?
2 Are there any special ideas that stand out for you in this poem? Why?

Reviewing

Reflect on the non-fiction texts you've read in this chapter

Talk about the texts you engaged with in this chapter.
- Which texts did you like and which didn't you like?
- Which do you think were well-written and why?
- What techniques did the writers use to create effects in their writing?
- What texts have you read that are similar to these?

If you like reading non-fiction, try these books:
- *I am Malala* by Malala Yousafzai
- *The Diary of a Young Girl* by Anne Frank
- *Eco Stories for Those Who Dare to Care* by Ben Hubbard
- *Unbelievable Football: The Most Incredible True Football Stories* by Matt Oldfield
- *Becoming* by Michelle Obama

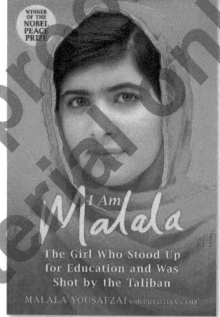

Reflect on your learning in this chapter

- What techniques have you learned to improve your reading, listening and speaking and writing?
- Make a list of things that you still need to master – or concepts with which you need more practice.
  - Compile a plan for tackling these.
  - Discuss your lists and ideas with your classmates and your teacher.

DESCRIPTIVE WRITING

Reading
★ Extracts from novels that describe characters, animals, places, houses and scenes

Speaking and listening
★ Listening to descriptions of places
★ Describing characters through dialogue
★ Verbal and non-verbal communication
★ Discussing characters

Writing
★ Techniques for descriptive writing
★ Describing a night-time scene

Key skills
★ Choice of words
★ An author's voice
★ Simple, compound and complex sentences
★ Connectives

LET'S TALK

Find a few examples of descriptive writing.

■ Where did you find them? Are they in fiction or non-fiction texts?

■ Which descriptions let you see, hear, feel, smell or taste what is being described? What kind of language does the author use to do that? What words does the author use to put you directly in the scene?

■ What features could you use in your own writing to improve it?

#349898079

Speaking and listening

Describing places

HINT

Look for pictures that could help you describe what heat feels like and describe them.

LET'S TALK

Work in a group. Talk about what it feels like to be hot. How do you feel? What do plants and other living things around you look like? What does the sky look like? What sounds can you hear? Quickly write down as many words as you can that describe what you feel and see. Share your ideas with other groups.

KEY WORDS

novel a work of fiction, usually written in a book

Activity 3.1

A High Wind in Jamaica is a **novel** by Richard Hughes which deals with the accidental kidnapping of a group of English children by pirates. Listen to an extract in which the writer describes the heat the children experience in a scene.

Work in a pair. Read the questions below, then listen again and make a few notes as you listen to help answer the questions.

1   What is the setting in this extract from the novel?
2   How did the heat affect the children?
3   How does the setting echo what the children are feeling?
4   Which animals are described in the extract and how do they react to the heat?
5   Later in the day, a hurricane hits the area. How do the descriptions in the extract suggest that something serious is about to happen?

WORD ATTACK SKILLS

The author has chosen the words in the description carefully. Look at the underlined words in each of the phrases and sentences below.

The morning <u>advanced</u>.

the insects were too <u>lethargic</u> to pipe

the <u>basking</u> lizards hid themselves and panted

The children <u>ceased</u> even to think.

1   Discuss with your partner what these words mean. You can role-play them. Talk about why the author used them. Which other words could he have used? Which word is more effective?

Reading

Describing scenes

▲ The character Mma Precious Ramotswe is a detective in Botswana created by Alexander McCall Smith.

Author: Alexander McCall Smith

Alexander McCall Smith has written in many forms. *The No. 1 Ladies' Detective Agency* is a series of novels set in Botswana that feature the character Mma Precious Ramotswe.

Extract: *The No. 1 Ladies' Detective Agency*

Suddenly she saw the house, tucked away behind the trees almost in the shadow of the hill. It was a bare earth house in the traditional style; brown mud walls, a few **glassless** windows, with a knee-height wall around the yard. A previous owner, a long time ago, had painted designs on the wall, but neglect and the years had scaled them off and only their ghosts remained …

She opened the door and eased herself out of the van. The sun was riding high; its light prickled at her skin. They were too far west here, too close to the Kalahari Desert, and her unease increased. This was not the comforting land she had grown up with; this was the **merciless** Africa, the **waterless** land.

Alexander McCall Smith

Spotlight on: descriptions of places in novels

Writers set the scene for events in stories and use descriptions of places to add meaning to the events in a story. Choosing words carefully can help to create a meaningful setting too.

EXERCISE 3.1

Read the extract from *The No. 1 Ladies' Detective Agency* above. The detective, Mma Ramotswe, is investigating a murder. In this scene she arrives at the house of the suspected murderer.

1   Choose three words or phrases that suggest that the house and its surroundings were unwelcoming and hostile. Give reasons for your choice.

2   Explain the effects of the sun on Mma Ramotswe in the extract.

3   How does the description of the house and its surroundings emphasise that this is a serious crime?

Activity 3.2

Read the extract again and discuss how the author uses language, punctuation and word choice.

1   What is the effect of the first word in the opening sentence?

2   How does the description of the setting enhance the unease felt by the character?

3   The author uses several adjectives that end in *-less* in this extract (*glassless*, *merciless*, *waterless*). What is the author trying to emphasise?

4   Why does the author use a semi-colon in the second line and an ellipsis at the end of the first paragraph?

LONG PAGE

39

KEY WORD

compound adjective
an adjective made up
of two or more words,
often with a hyphen
between the words

Activity 3.3

Work in a pair. Read
the extract from
*A High Wind in
Jamaica* again.

1 Find as many
example of
pronouns as you
can.

2 Discuss which
nouns these
pronouns
replace.

Spelling

Adjectives often
end in *-able*, *-ible*,
-ful, *-ish*, *-less*
or *-y*. They can
also end in *-ing*
and *-ed*. You can
make adjectives
from other words
by adding these
suffixes.
Sometimes you
need to change
a word ending to
add the suffix. For
example, mercy –
merciless, gurgle –
gurgling.
A compound
adjective often, but
not always, has a
hyphen.

Key skills

Choice of words

In the extracts from *A High Wind in Jamaica* and *The No. 1 Ladies'
Detective Agency*, you started to explore how the writers' choice of words
can have an impact on the reader. Writers can use adjectives, nouns, verbs
and adverbs to good effect!

Adjectives

Adjectives can describe colours, features and feelings. Writers use adjectives
in the same way that an artist uses paint or clay – to create.

We can use more than one adjective in a description and we can make
compound adjectives from two words as well. Look at these examples:

the <u>basking</u> lizards hid themselves (one adjective)

close over the ground a <u>dirty grey</u> haze hovered (two adjectives)

a <u>fair-sized</u> spring had bubbled up by the roadside (compound adjective
with hyphen)

Verbs

Verbs describe actions. Verbs can also help writers to create pictures in the
mind of a reader. They help to create a scene or to develop a character in a
story. Look at these examples:

a fair-sized spring had <u>bubbled</u> up by the roadside

it was dry again, although <u>gurgling</u> inwardly to itself.

She <u>eased</u> herself out of the van.

The sun <u>was riding</u> high; its light <u>prickled</u> at her skin.

LET'S TALK

- In a pair, list five different lively
  verbs you could use to describe
  how a character runs, talks and
  laughs (for example, rushes,
  whispers, chuckles).

- Think of what may happen next
  after the scene in *The No. 1 Ladies'
  Detective Agency*. Write five
  sentences using lively verbs. Share
  your sentences with other pairs.

EXERCISE 3.2

1 Write a short description of a very hot day. Write at least four sentences with
well-chosen adjectives and verbs. The adjectives and verbs should help
reflect what the day feels and looks like. You can use some of the words you
wrote down earlier.

2 Check your spelling. Make sure you have spelled tricky common words
correctly. For example: light (not lite), were (not wear or where) etc.

Reading and speaking

Describing animals

Author: Gerald Durrell

He wrote three autobiographical novels about his time in Corfu, Greece with his family. The first extract you will read is from the second book, *Birds, Beasts and Relatives*.

WORD ATTACK SKILLS

Work out the meanings of the following words from the context and from what you know about word families.

- ✔ determination
- ✔ hedgerows
- ✔ crew-cut
- ✔ overfeed
- ✔ excursions

LET'S TALK

Talk about the extract you read and discuss how Gerald Durrell uses words to describe the hedgehogs.

1   Find adjectives which describe what they look like, and verbs which describe how they behave.

2   Which words made the description lively, effective and painted a good picture for you?

Extract: *Birds, Beasts and Relatives*

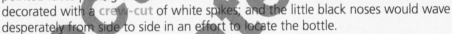

They are covered with a thick coating of spikes but these are white and soft, as though made of rubber. They gradually harden and turn brown when the babies are a few weeks old. When they are old enough to leave the nursery the mother leads them out and shows them how to hunt for food; they walk in line, the tail of one held in the mouth of the baby behind. The baby at the head of the column holds tight to mother's tail with grim **determination**, and they move through the twilit **hedgerows** like a strange prickly centipede …

Mine were always ready for food at any hour of the day or night. You had only to touch the box and a chorus of shrill screams arose from four little pointed faces poking out of the leaves, each head decorated with a **crew-cut** of white spikes; and the little black noses would wave desperately from side to side in an effort to locate the bottle.

Most baby animals know when they have had enough, but in my experience this does not apply to baby hedgehogs. Like four survivors from a raft, they flung themselves on to the bottle and sucked and sucked and sucked as though they had not had a decent meal in weeks. If I had allowed it they would have drunk twice as much as was good for them. As it was, I think I tended to **overfeed** them, for their tiny legs could not support the weight of their fat bodies, and they would advance across the carpet with a curious swimming motion, their tummies dragging on the ground. However, they progressed very well: their legs grew stronger, their eyes opened, and they would even make daring **excursions** as much as 15 centimetres away from their box.

Alexander McCall Smith

EXERCISE 3.2

1   Write down six facts about hedgehogs.

2   Choose four words or phrases that refer to the hedgehogs as if they were human children. How do these expressions help you to imagine the appearance and behaviour of the animals?

3   Explain, using your own words, the way in which the hedgehogs drank from the bottle of milk.

4   Explain the effect of having drunk too much milk on the hedgehogs.

Reading, speaking and writing

Describing a house

The next extract is from the first book in Gerald Durrell's trilogy about living in Corfu: *My Family and Other Animals*. In this extract he describes the appearance of the villa in which he and his family lived.

EXERCISE 3.4

Read the description in the extract.

1   Read it once and make notes for yourself about the different things that are described in order to get the main ideas. You do not need to understand every word.
    For example:

    where the house is: on a slope, with cypress trees

    what it looks like: square, with a garden

2   Then read the description again and add more details to your notes, for example, about plants in the garden and colours.

Extract: *My Family and Other Animals*

Halfway up the slope, guarded by a group of tall, slim, cypress-trees, nestled a small strawberry-pink villa, like some exotic fruit lying in the greenery. The cypress-trees undulated gently in the breeze, as if they were busily painting the sky a still brighter blue for our arrival.

The villa was small and square, standing in its tiny garden with an air of pink-faced determination. Its shutters had been faded by the sun to a delicate creamy-green, cracked and bubbled in places. The garden, surrounded by tall fuchsia hedges, had the flower beds worked in complicated geometrical patterns, marked with smooth white stones. The white cobbled paths, scarcely as wide as a rake's head, wound laboriously round beds hardly larger than a big straw hat, beds in the shape of stars, half-moons, triangles, and circles all overgrown with a shaggy tangle of flowers run wild. Roses dropped petals that seemed as big and smooth as saucers, flame-red, moon-white, glossy, and unwrinkled; marigolds like broods of shaggy suns stood watching their parent's progress through the sky. In the low growth the pansies pushed their velvety, innocent faces through the leaves, and the violets drooped sorrowfully under their heart-shaped leaves. The bougainvillaea that sprawled luxuriously over the tiny iron balcony was hung, as though for a carnival, with its lantern-shaped magenta flowers. In the darkness of the fuchsia-hedge a thousand ballerina-like blooms quivered expectantly. The warm air was thick with the scent of a hundred dying flowers, and full of the gentle, soothing whisper and murmur of insects.

Gerald Durrell

EXTENSION

Find a picture online that matches the description of the villa in the extract or draw one of your own. Compare your pictures with those of your partner or group. What did you get right? What details could you still add?

EXERCISE 3.5

1 Write a paragraph in which you describe a house or garden that you know well. Write 4 or 5 sentences. Use some of the compound adjectives you have read or made up in the previous activity.

2 Read your descriptions aloud to your partner or group.

KEY WORDS

voice an author's unique style of writing
personality what a person's character and behaviour are like

Activity 3.4

Gerald Durrell uses several compound adjectives in the extract from *My Family and Other Animals*. Work in a pair to answer these questions.

1 Find five compound adjectives in the extract.
2 Discuss which words the author uses to make each adjective, what each adjective means and which nouns they describe.
3 Use each compound adjective in a sentence of your own to describe something that you know well.

Key skills

An author's voice

Most authors develop a distinctive voice in their writing. You will begin to recognise an author's **voice** once you have read several pieces of writing by the same author.

What is the 'voice'?

You can think of voice as a style of writing that makes the writing unique or special. An author can create this voice through their choice of words, types of sentence structure, and using formal or informal language.

Gerald Durrell, for example, describes the appearance of his home and his animals in great detail, using lots of descriptive adjectives. If you read more of his book *My Family and Other Animals*, you will see that he also adopts a humorous tone in his writing as he finds the actions of his family and his animals quite amusing.

In an autobiography, in which an author writes about her or his own life, we may begin to understand something about the **personality** of the author. Gerald Durrell reveals his love for animals in his writing as he describes how he observes and cares for them.

LET'S TALK

Discuss Gerald Durrell's distinctive voice. Could you recognise his voice (his style of writing) from the two extracts you have read? Look at the language that he uses and give examples to support your answer.

Revise simple, compound and complex sentences

Do you remember the difference between simple, compound and complex sentences? A **simple sentence** is a sentence with only one independent clause. It only has one verb and it usually has a subject. It is an effective way of making a short, clear statement. It can add drama to a scene and make the reader stop and pay attention.

> The villa <u>was</u> small, pink and square.
>
> Suddenly everything <u>was</u> silent.

However, simple sentences can also have phrases added to them. **Phrases** are groups of words with no verb or subject. Many writers use phrases to add details in simple sentences.

> It was a bare earth house <u>in the traditional style; brown mud walls, a few glassless windows, with a knee-height wall around the yard</u>.

A dependent clause can describe the independent clause, help to describe a sequence of events or even give an explanation or reason for an event.

> Roses <u>dropped</u> petals that <u>seemed</u> as big and smooth as saucers.
>
> Most baby animals <u>know</u> when they <u>have had</u> enough.

A **compound sentence** has two or more main (independent) clauses. Sometimes the two clauses express a contrast.

> It <u>rained</u> for a few minutes but soon it <u>was</u> dry again.
>
> She <u>opened</u> the door and <u>eased</u> herself out of the van.

The clauses in complex and compound sentences are linked by **connectives** which help to describe the relationship between the clauses. Clauses can also be linked by punctuation marks.

EXERCISE 3.6

Look at the photographs below. Choose one of the photographs.

1   Write two simple sentences to describe the photo.

2   Add at least one phrase to each sentence. The phrase can describe the subject, the verb or the object of your sentence. Think about the effect that you want to achieve.

3   Add a clause to each sentence. Note whether you have written a complex or a compound sentence.

HINT

A **complex sentence** has one main (independent) and at least one dependent (or subordinate) **clause**.

KEY WORDS

simple sentence a sentence with only one independent clause

clause a group of words that includes a verb

compound sentence a sentence with two or more main (independent) clauses

complex sentence a sentence with one main clause and at least one dependent clause

connective any word that links clauses, sentences or ideas together

Building up detail in descriptions

Word choice is one way in which writers can build pictures for their readers. Writers can also use literary devices such as **similes** to add details. Here are some examples from *My Family and Other Animals* (page 42).

a small strawberry-pink villa, like some exotic fruit lying in the greenery

the cypress-trees undulated gently in the breeze, <u>as if they were busily painting the sky</u>

The length of sentences and different sentence openings can also be used to add details and interest to descriptions. Writers can use phrases as well as compound or complex sentences to add details. Gerald Durrell uses long sentences with phrases and several clauses in each.

Look at how the writer has built up information in this sentence from *My Family and Other Animals*.

Halfway up the slope, guarded by a group of tall, slim, cypress-trees, nestled a small strawberry-pink villa, like some exotic fruit lying in the greenery.

The sentence begins with a short phrase.

This is the main clause in the sentence.

This comparison (another simile) adds information.

Activity 3.5

Work in a pair. Read the texts by Gerald Durrell again.
1   Find two examples of sentences in which the author has used different ways of building up details.
2   Read your sentences to another pair and explain how they have been written.

EXERCISE 3.7

Look at the paragraph you wrote of Exercise 3.5 again. Now try to add details to the paragraph.
1   Extend one sentence by adding a phrase at the beginning or at the end.
2   Include one simile in a phrase or a clause.
3   Add one more clause to one of the sentences to make it a compound or a complex sentence.

Reading and speaking

Describing a character

In the next two extracts, you will read and explore how writers describe characters. Both extracts have an historical context.

Author: Mary Seacole

Mary Seacole was born in 1805 in Jamaica. Although she had no formal training as a nurse, she learned healing and medical skills from her mother. She became well-known for her work as a nurse during the Crimean War. She wrote an autobiography, published in 1857, which described her childhood and the places she visited and worked.

GLOSSARY

blandishment actions or words which can be meant to persuade and flatter

prevalent widespread, common at a particular time

WORD ATTACK SKILLS

Use your knowledge of word families to work out the meanings of the following words:

✔ doctress
✔ repute
✔ patroness

LET'S TALK

Work in a group and discuss these questions.

1 What impression do you have of Mary from this extract? Think about the way she plays with her doll.

Activity 3.6

1 What do you know about how authors describe and develop characters in stories? Share your ideas in a group. In an autobiography, the authors describe themselves and how they behave and feel. They may also include scenes that reveal much about their own characters.

2 Read the extract from *Adventures of Mrs Seacole in Many Lands*, in which Mary describes part of her childhood and how she developed an interest in medicine.

Extract: Adventures of Mrs Seacole in Many Lands

It is not my intention to dwell at any length upon the recollections of my childhood. My mother kept a boarding-house in Kingston, and was, like very many of the Creole women, an admirable **doctress**; in high **repute** with the officers of both services, and their wives, who were from time to time stationed at Kingston. It was very natural that I should inherit her tastes; and so I had from early youth a yearning for medical knowledge and practice which has never deserted me. When I was a very young child I was taken by an old lady, who brought me up in her household among her own grandchildren, and who could scarcely have shown me more kindness had I been one of them; indeed, I was so spoiled by my kind **patroness** that, but for being frequently with my mother, I might very likely have grown up idle and useless. But I saw so much of her, and of her patients, that the ambition to become a doctress early took firm root in my mind; and I was very young when I began to make use of the little knowledge I had acquired from watching my mother, upon a great sufferer—my doll. I have

OVERMATTER

Describing a character

The next extract, from Charles Dickens, has a different historical context. The Victorian period was a time in which the British Empire was very powerful but society was based on the class to which you belonged.

EXERCISE 3.8

Use any reading strategies you know to read the extract from *Hard Times*. You may need to read it more than once.

Author: Charles Dickens

Charles Dickens (1812–1870) is often regarded as the greatest novelist of his time. His many novels include *Oliver Twist*, *A Christmas Carol* and *Great Expectations*.

Extract: *Hard Times*

He was a rich man: banker, merchant, manufacturer, and what not. A big, loud man, with a stare, and a metallic laugh. A man made out of a coarse material, which seemed to have been stretched to make so much of him. A man with a great puffed head and forehead, swelled veins in his **temples**, and such a strained skin to his face that it seemed to hold his eyes open, and lift his eyebrows up. A man with a **pervading** appearance on him of being inflated like a balloon, and ready to start. A man who could never sufficiently **vaunt** himself a self-made man. A man who was always proclaiming, through that brassy speaking-trumpet of a voice of his, his old ignorance and his old poverty. A man who was the Bully of humility.

… Mr Bounderby looked older; his seven or eight and forty might have had the seven or eight added to it again, without surprising anybody. He had not much hair. One might have fancied he had talked it off; and that what was left, all standing up in disorder, was in that condition from being constantly blown about by his windy boastfulness.

Charles Dickens

Spotlight on: historical context

Historical context is influenced by the trends and events of the time in which events happen. Politics, economics, social behaviour and culture have an effect on this context. Mary Seacole was influenced by the times she lived in. She worked as a healer/nurse from an early age without formal training. This was part of her culture.

EXERCISE 3.9

1 How old is Mr Bounderby in the extract above?
2 What do you think the phrase 'metallic laugh' suggests about Mr Bounderby and his interests?
3 Choose four words or phrases that suggest Mr Bounderby is not a nice man. How do your chosen phrases show this?
4 Explain what is meant by 'the Bully of humility'.
5 Choose two descriptions that suggest that the writer is making fun of Mr Bounderby. Explain the reasons for your choice.

LET'S TALK

1 Dickens was a social commentator. Do you think his purpose may have been to comment on Victorian society? What makes you say so?
2 Describe the register (of the language) in this extract. Would you use language like this to describe a person? How is the register related to the historical context?
3 Now compare this extract with the extract from Mary Seacole's autobiography. What are the similarities and differences?

WORD ATTACK SKILLS

Look up the meaning of the highlighted words.
✔ temples
✔ pervading
✔ vaunt

LONG PAGE

Reading

Reading descriptions aloud

Author: Flann O'Brien

Flann O'Brien was a penname of Brian O'Nolan (1911-1966), an Irish novelist and playwright. *The Third Policeman* was only published after his death in 1967.

WORD ATTACK SKILLS

Work out the meanings of the words in bold from your understanding of word families and from the context:
- ✔ weed-tufted
- ✔ derelict
- ✔ clambered
- ✔ stretchings

LET'S TALK

This scene is in the first person, from the point of view of the main character. Think about the effect that this has on the reader.

1 Try telling part of story to someone else in the third person. Start like this: 'He/She opened the door and walked as softly as he could...'

2 Then compare the stories.
- ▪ Which version do you think is the most real and exciting?
- ▪ Which version makes you feel part of the story?

Activity 3.7

Read the following description with a partner. As you read, try to read ahead and think about what is happening. Try to reflect this in your reading.

Extract: *The Third Policeman*

I opened the iron gate and walked as softly as I could up the **weed-tufted** gravel drive. My mind was strangely empty. I felt no glow of pleasure and was unexcited at the prospect of becoming rich. I was occupied only with the mechanical task of finding a black box.

The front door was closed and set far back in a very deep porch. The wind and rain had whipped a coating of gritty dust against the panels and deep into the crack where the door opened, showing that it had been shut for years. Standing on a **derelict** flower-bed, I tried to push open the first window on the left. It yielded to my strength, raspingly and stubbornly. I **clambered** through the opening and found myself, not at once in a room, but crawling along the deepest window-ledge I had ever seen. After I had jumped noisily down upon the floor, I looked up and the open window seemed very far away and much too small to have admitted me.

The room where I found myself was thick with dust, musty and empty of all furniture. Spiders had erected great **stretchings** of their web about the fireplace. I made my way quickly to the hall, threw open the door of the room where the box was and paused on the threshold. It was a dark morning and the weather had stained the windows with blears of grey wash which kept the brightest part of the weak light from coming in. The far corner of the room was a blur of shadow. I had a sudden urge to have done with my task and be out of this house forever.

Flann O'Brien

EXERCISE 3.10

1 Where does the narrator of the story first land once he has climbed through the window?

2 What evidence can you find in the second paragraph that the house has 'been shut for years'?

3 Why is it difficult for the narrator to see into the far corner of the room in the final paragraph?

4 What evidence is there that the inside of the house is deserted?

5 Choose five words or phrases that suggest to you that there is something

HINT
Other connectives that are useful for sequencing are *first*, *before*, *then* and *when*.

Key skills

Connectives

Connectives link clauses and show us the relationship between the information in the clauses. They can also help to add detail to descriptions.

Some conntectives help to give readers an idea of the sequence of events being described. Look at this example from *The Third Policeman*.

> I opened the iron gate and walked as softly as I could up the weed-tufted gravel drive.
> After I had jumped noisily down upon the floor, I looked up and the open window seemed very far away and much too small to have admitted me.

Activity 3.8

Work with a partner and discuss how to connect some of the following sentences to make a paragraph in which the sequence of events is clear. You can change the verb tenses and other words in the sentences.

- He stopped and looked at the house carefully.
- He walked down the drive towards the house.
- He knocked at the door but no one answered.
- He climbed through a window to get into the house.

Adverbs

KEY WORD

adverb a word, frequently ending in *-ly*, that is used to describe the action expressed by a verb, e.g. Joe ate *hungrily*.

An **adverb** describes or adds to the meaning of a verb, an adjective or another adverb. Adverbs make descriptions stronger because they help to create descriptive phrases. Look at these examples:

My mind was strangely empty. (*strangely* is an adverb that modifies an adjective)
They progressed very well. (*very* is an adverb that modifies another adverb, *well*)

EXERCISE 3.11

1 Add an adverb to each of these sentences to add detail to each description.
   a She made her way down the street.
   b The leaves of the trees moved in the breeze.
   c The house is far away.
   d The house was quiet.

2 Copy these sentences from *My Family and Other Animals*.

> The cypress-trees undulated gently in the breeze, as if they were busily painting the sky a still brighter blue for our arrival. The white cobbled paths ... wound laboriously round beds hardly larger than a big straw hat

   a Underline the adverbs and identify the words that they describe.
   b Replace each adverb with another adverb that has a similar meaning.

Author: William Golding

William Golding (1911-1993) was a British novelist, playwright and poet. He received the Nobel Prize for Literature in 1983.

LET'S TALK

The two characters in this extract have just met each other after the crash. Look at their opening exchanges. What does the reader learn about them?

LONG PAGE

Listening and speaking

Describing characters through dialogue

Lord of the Flies is about a group of schoolboys who have to survive on a tropical island after the plane in which they are travelling crashes.

EXERCISE 3.12

1 Listen to the extract from *Lord of the Flies*. Try to identify the characters in this extract as you listen and start to form an idea of them from the way they speak.

2 Read the extract silently. Make notes of anything you do not understand. Discuss these notes with a partner.

Extract: *Lord of the Flies*

The fair boy was peering at the reef through screwed-up eyes.

'All them other kids,' the fat boy went on. 'Some of them must have got out. They must have, mustn't they?'

The fair boy began to pick his way as casually as possible toward the water. He tried to be offhand and not too obviously uninterested, but the fat boy hurried after him.

'Aren't there any grown-ups at all?'

'I don't think so.'

The fair boy said this solemnly; but then the delight of a realized ambition overcame him. In the middle of the scar he stood on his head and grinned at the reversed fat boy.

'No grown-ups!'

The fat boy thought for a moment.

'That pilot.'

The fair boy allowed his feet to come down and sat on the steamy earth.

'He must have flown off after he dropped us. He couldn't land there. Not in a plane with wheels.'

'We were attacked!'

'He'll be back all right.'

The fat boy shook his head.

'When we were coming down I looked through one of the windows. I saw the other part of the plane. There were flames coming out of it.'

He looked up and down the scar.

'And this is what the cabin done.'

The fair boy reached out and touched the jagged end of a trunk. For a moment he looked interested.

'What happened to it?' he asked. 'Where's it got to now?'

'That storm dragged it out to sea. It wasn't half dangerous with all them tree trunks falling. There must have been some kids still in it.'

He hesitated for a moment, and then spoke again.

'What's your name?'

'Ralph.'

William Golding

Reading and speaking

Verbal and non-verbal communication

EXERCISE 3.13

1. What do the manner, actions and direct speech of the 'fair boy' tell us about his character?

2. What does the 'fat boy' say about what happened to the plane?

3. Do you think the boys' direct speech and the way they talk to each other sounds like everyday conversation? Explain your answer by referring to words or phrases they use.

4. We are told, 'He hesitated for a moment, and then spoke again.' Who hesitated? Who is Ralph?

5. Find two examples of different words that are used to introduce the direct speech.

6. What technique is used to make the direct speech more interesting? Give an example from the extract.

> **Activity 3.9**
>
> In a group of three, role-play the extract from *Lord of the Flies*. One person is the narrator, one person is 'fat boy' and the other 'fair boy'. Think about how the words are, the non-verbal communication and how the characters move.

In everyday speech, describing a person in spoken words or orally is slightly different from writing about them descriptively. Usually in our oral descriptions we use simple, clear and accurate descriptions and appropriate language rather than figures of speech like similes and metaphors.

We provide as many factual details as possible, such as:

- gender, ethnicity or race (if relevant)
- approximate age, height, size or weight
- what they are wearing
- facial features, like eye colour, hair colour, length and style.

We also give any details that stand out, for example, if they wear glasses, have a beard, tattoo or scar. We may describe how they walk, talk, stand and if they have any strange mannerisms like a nervous twitch.

> **HINT**
> The key to giving a good description of a person is to be observant. This means that you pay attention and notice their special details and features. Listen to what they say and how they say it. Notice their mood and behaviour. Use your five senses.

> **Activity 3.10**
>
> Imagine that you have been witness to a minor crime and that you are helping the police with their enquiries by giving them a description of the person or persons involved. Give your description to your group – you should base it on someone you all know (although not necessarily a member of the group) – and ask them to see if they can guess who you are describing. Remember: you wouldn't know the criminal's name!

EXERCISE 3.14

Choose one of the extracts and read it aloud to your class or group.

Remember to:

- speak loudly enough so that the audience can hear you
- use voices for the characters: think about their accent or tone
- look up occasionally to make eye contact with your audience

LONG PAGE

Writing

Descriptions

Techniques for descriptive writing

Describing things effectively is an important way to directly involve your readers – the more convincing your descriptions, the more likely you are to draw your readers in. It's important that you make your descriptions as clear as possible by focusing on specific details of the person or place that you are describing.

An effective and straightforward way of including such detail is by appealing to the different senses. Ask yourself the following questions before you start to write to help you focus on these details.

- What does the person or place look like?
- What sounds do I hear? (This could refer to a person's voice and/or movements, or to the sounds that are most apparent in the place you are writing about.)
- What does it feel like? (For example, you could describe a character's handshake or the feeling of damp and cold in a winter scene.)
- What does it taste like?
- What does it smell like?

Most importantly, good descriptive writing depends on choosing exactly the right word to communicate what is in your mind. It's usually better to present your description in a dynamic way through an effective choice of verbs and adverbs, rather than disrupting your description with too many adjectives and similes. For example, instead of writing 'the car was as clean as a whistle', you could write 'the car was cleaned so thoroughly, not a single speck of dirt could be found on its immaculate paint and sparkling windows'. This gives the reader more detail and may also hint at the behaviour of the character who owns the car.

Activity 3.11

With a partner, read through the extracts from *Hard Times* and *My Family and Other Animals* again, and make notes on the ways in which the writers describe the places and the effect it has on the reader. Copy and complete the following table. The first example has been done for you.

Add three more for each extract.

Hard Times	
Detail – words or phrases used	**Effect they have on the reader (image created)**
'a man made out of coarse material'	makes the reader dislike the character, think badly of the character
My Family and Other Animals	

LONG PAGE

1. Work in a group. Think about the extracts you have read and listened to in this unit. Make notes about the ways in which authors create good descriptions. Think about the structure of sentences and vocabulary, for example. Find examples and share your ideas with another group.
2. Read and discuss the notes about descriptive writing below.

HINT

Think of how you can use the grammatical structure of your sentences to build up detail in these paragraphs.

EXERCISE 3.15

Here are some brief notes made by a writer about what is to be included in a description of a scene.

Night-time; house; trees; countryside; people entering house; cars; moonlight; noises in background; people talking; food being cooked; man in shadow of tree; games

Write two short paragraphs in which you develop these notes to produce a detailed and vivid description.

You could also use these photographs to help you.

Through choosing your words carefully, try to create a warm and welcoming atmosphere in one of the paragraphs and then a sinister and threatening atmosphere in your other paragraph.

EXERCISE 3.16

Write two longer paragraphs in which you do the following:

1 Describe an unusual and eccentric character. It may help to base this character on someone you know, but you can, of course, add or make up details. It doesn't have to be a human being – it could be a pet or another animal. You could use one of the characters you have read about in this chapter.

2 Describe the place in which this character lives. You should concentrate on creating a description of a place that matches the eccentric nature of the character you have described in the previous paragraph.

You could also use the photographs on the left to give you ideas.

SELF-CHECK

■ Is your spelling correct? Use your knowledge of word families and how to add suffixes to words.

■ Have you chosen interesting words to describe your character?

■ Have you tried to vary the types of sentences you have used – simple and complex or compound?

■ Have you built up details by adding clauses and phrases in your sentences?

Reviewing

Reflect on the non-fiction texts you've read in this chapter

Talk about:

- which texts you liked and which you didn't like
- which you think were well-written and why
- what techniques the writers used to create effects in their writing
- what texts you have read that are similar to these.

If you liked reading the extracts from these authors, try reading the full books or their other books, such as:

- Books by Charles Dickens: *Oliver Twist, A Christmas Carol, David Copperfield, A Tale of Two Cities* and *Great Expectations*
- Books by Alexander McCall Smith: *The No. 1 Ladies' Detective Agency: Tears of the Giraffe, Morality for Beautiful Girls, The Kalahari Typing School for Men, The Full Cupboard of Life, In the Company of Cheerful Ladies* (also known as *The Night-Time Dancer*), *Blue Shoes and Happiness, The Miracle at Speedy Motors*

You could also try:

- *Skellig* by David Almond
- *The Graveyard Book* by Neil Gaiman
- *Planet Omar: Accidental Trouble Magnet* by Zanib Mian
- *The Island at the End of Everything* by Kiran Millwood Hargrave
- *Northern Lights* by Philip Pullman
- *Oranges in No Man's Land* by Elizabeth Laird
- *Some Places More Than Others* by Renée Watson

LET'S TALK

Think about all the ways in which you have learned to describe places, characters and events. Which can you use to develop your writing?

Reflect on your learning in this chapter

- What techniques have you learned to improve your descriptive writing?
- Make a list of things that you still need to master – or concepts with which you need more practice.
  - Compile a plan for tackling these.
  - Discuss your lists and ideas with a partner and your teacher.

4 Endangered!

Reading

★ Newspaper articles
★ Magazine articles
★ Advertisements
★ Emotive language
★ Identifying bias, opinion and fact

Speaking and listening

★ Discussing environmental issues
★ Holding a class debate about an environmental issue
★ Making a video for an online campaign on an important current issue

ENDANGERED!

Writing

★ Using spelling patterns
★ Snappy slogans
★ An online campaign about an important issue
★ Formal or business letters

Key skills

★ Punctuation: apostrophes
★ Word families, prefixes and vocabulary
★ Verb phrases
★ Building detail in sentences
★ Using modal adverbs in persuasive language

LET'S TALK

Non-fiction writing takes many forms. In Chapter 1, we looked at some straightforward types of factual texts. In this chapter, we look at non-fiction texts that are written to persuade and influence people.

Look at a few texts found in newspapers, magazines and on websites.

■ Is it easy to identify fiction and non-fiction texts?

■ What is the purpose of these different texts?

■ What is the point of view of the author in these texts?

■ Do you agree or disagree with the authors' point of view? Are there any words or phrases they have used that informed your decision?

Writing

Using spelling patterns

The theme of this chapter is environmental issues, including endangered animals.

Notice that environmental and endangered share a spelling pattern. Spellers often make mistakes following spelling patterns with words beginning:

- en
- em
- in
- im

Read through the lists of words.

environment	emancipate	insure	important
endangered	empower	inquire	imperative
endure	embrace	inspire	impossible
encourage	embark	inequality	imperfect
engage		interfere	

Activity 4.1

Work with a partner. Sort the words into a diagram like this:

I know the meaning of these words

I know how to spell these words

Use a dictionary to find the meaning of each word you do not know. Choose five words you need to learn and write sentences that include these words.

For example:
embrace – to hug or accept enthusiastically
To help save the planet, people should embrace recycling.

Memes and messaging

Humorous or cultural messages are common in advertising. Popular images with text may 'go viral' or become known as 'memes' which are often shared many times on social media.

Visual messaging like this is powerful, and influences people's beliefs and opinions.

The purpose of visual messaging can be:

- to persuade
- to sell
- to manipulate
- to hide the truth
- to raise awareness.

LET'S TALK

What is the purpose of the visual message on the right? Discuss the choice of language – how is it designed to meet its purpose?

This baby has already lost its mother ...

... don't let it lose its entire species!

Show your support at www.savetheorangutan.org

Speaking and listening

Environmental issues are some of the most important facing the world.

Activity 4.2

In a group, discuss the following questions on the theme of environmental issues.
- What do you know?
- What do you believe?
- What questions do you have?

Take on different roles in your group:
- Lead – your role is to make sure everyone can contribute equally.
- Speaker – take it in turns to share your knowledge and beliefs.
- Listener – listen carefully, and wait until the speaker has finished before you ask questions.
- Summariser – make notes and report back the main ideas to the group at the end.

Afterwards, share your group's main findings with the whole class.

Key skills

Punctuation – apostrophes

Apostrophes are used for two main purposes:

1 To show when a letter or letters have been missed out of a word (when a word or words have been contracted). For example:

<u>Don't</u> let it lose its entire species! I <u>didn't</u> understand that. <u>It's</u> not fair. They <u>weren't</u> paying attention.

2 To show possession, as follows:

a In the singular, the possessive form is made by adding an apostrophe before the -s ('s). For example:

an orang-utan's habitat

b When the plural form of a noun is made by adding -s to the singular, the possessive is shown by adding an apostrophe after the -s (s'). For example:

the orang-utans' habitat

c In irregular plural forms, when the plural form of a noun is not made by adding -s, the possessive is shown by adding 's. For example:

men: the men's department

children: the children's drawings

women: the women's race

An apostrophe is required in expressions such as *a month's wait, a week's holiday* or *an hour's journey*.

> **KEY WORD**
> **apostrophe** a punctuation mark (') indicating possession or omission

> **HINT**
>
> **It's** a hot and humid place. (It's = It is)
>
> This baby has already lost its mother. (**its** = belonging to it)
>
> **He's/She's** a babysitter.
>
> This is **his** mother.

▲ Borneo is a hot and humid place

EXERCISE 4.1

Rewrite these sentences, using apostrophes where necessary.

1 A baby orang-utan became an emblem of the urgent crisis facing Borneos endangered orang-utans.

2 Holding hands with an orang-utan feels like holding a childs hand.

3 What destroys the orang-utans habitat?

4 Its very expensive to rehabilitate an orang-utan and monitor its progress.

5 Cant we do something to help the orang-utans?

6 Whats that place? Thats a jungle school where the orang-utans learn to climb trees and find food for themselves.

Writing

Create some snappy slogans

The messages of advertising are short and snappy, but they do not tell us the facts.

Some people prefer to only read messages they agree with already.

This can cause disagreements between different groups of people who hold different beliefs.

Activity 4.3

Work in groups and hold a class discussion debate on the following question:

What are the best sources of information to read, if you want to form a reasoned and informed opinion on important matters?

Effective advertisements:

- use strong and snappy headlines that draw attention and are memorable
- often use emotive language to create an emotional reaction in the reader
- have pictures, photographs or graphics that embellish the overall message
- use persuasive language to motivate action on the part of the reader, such as buying a product or service, or going to a website or shop
- build memorable products, services or brands.

Discuss any effective advertisements you have seen rrecently: what makes them good?

KEY WORD

emotive language words chosen to arouse feelings

LET'S TALK

Work with a partner to create some snappy advertising slogans on environmental themes. Make sure you use apostrophes correctly!

EXTENSION

Use a computer to design the slogans and add images.

Key skills

Word families, prefixes and vocabulary

Here are four topical vocabulary words, each using a prefix:

- deforestation
- disagreement
- international
- cooperation.

Discuss the words with a partner.
- What is the meaning of each word?
- What is the prefix?
- What would each word mean without its prefix?

Create a word family map for each word. Use a dictionary or appropriate online resource to help.

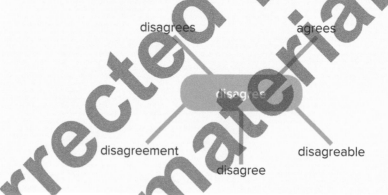

EXTENSION

Here are some of the most common prefixes found in English, along with their original meanings (be careful not to confuse the first two in the list).

Prefix	Meaning		Prefix	Meaning
ante-	before		pre-	before
anti-	against		re-	again
circum-	around		sub-	under
dis-	(not) opposite of		super-	above
fore-	before		trans-	across
in-, im-, il-, ir-	not		un-	not
inter-	between			

Use a dictionary to research other words that use prefixes. Try to find words that will be useful when speaking or writing about the topic of environmental issues.

Verb phrases

A verb phrase can be a main verb on its own, or it can be a main verb used with an auxiliary verb (such as *be, have, do*) and/or a **modal verb** (such as *can* or *would*). The main verbs always come last in the verb phrase.

Look at the underlined verb phrases in the following sentences, which are from extracts in this chapter.

> His habitat <u>has been destroyed</u>.
>
> Palm oil <u>can provide</u> vital livelihoods in an environmentally friendly way.
>
> In times past, the people of the jungle <u>would not kill</u> them.

Modal verbs can be used to add persuasive force to a sentence.

KEY WORD

modal verbs helping verbs or auxiliary verbs such as *can, may, will, could, should, would, shall, must, ought to* and *might*. They add meaning to the main verb in a sentence as they add possibility, ability, permission or obligation

Activity 4.5

Compare the force of each of these sentences.
A   We must protect the environment.
B   We could protect the environment.
C   We should protect the environment.
D   We might protect the environment.
E   We ought to protect the environment.
1   Discuss with a partner: how would you order these from most to least persuasive?
2   Go back to your environmental slogans. Rewrite them, including modal verbs to add persuasive force.

◀ Harvested palm oil fruits

KEY WORD

emotive language words chosen by writers deliberately to arouse feelings in their readers

Emotive language

Newspapers often use **emotive language**, both in their headlines and in their articles, to provoke their readers into supporting a certain point of view. It is a way of conveying opinions without making them obvious. They also may attempt to influence the responses of their readers by the choice of photographs accompanying their articles.

Why did the author choose to begin the article with this subheading? (Hint: think about the audience and purpose of the text.)

WORD ATTACK SKILLS

Using the context of the extract and the surrounding words, work out the meaning of emblem.

Activity 4.6

Read the following newspaper article. It is taken from a newspaper website (*The Scottish Sun*). It describes an establishment in Borneo where orang-utans are being trained to survive in the wild. As you read it, make a list of the emotive words.

Extract: School where pupils monkey around

His huge innocent eyes stare up mournfully

His habitat has been destroyed and his mother was left so disturbed after years in a tiny cage as a pet that she is unable to care for herself, let alone a baby.

▲ Furry nice to meet you ... Wigly greets *Sun* girl Emma Cox

Little Wigly has become an **emblem** of the urgent crisis facing Borneo's most famous resident, the orang-utan.

But amazingly, he is one of the lucky ones. At just three months old, he has not been so traumatised that he cannot learn the skills he will need to survive in the wild.

And his chances of being released into a safe area of the rainforest where he belongs look more hopeful than ever thanks to a ground-breaking project.

Emma Cox

The next extract is taken from a website about tigers.
The emotive language is mixed more carefully with factual sentences.

Extract: Tiger website

The plight of tigers in crisis

▲ The tiger is one of the most endangered species in the world

Since 1900, the endangered tigers' habitat and numbers have been reduced by up to 95 per cent. Poachers continue to poison waterholes or set steel wire snares to kill tigers and tiger prey, selling their skins and body parts for use in traditional medicine.

Despite 20 years of international conservation efforts, we are losing ground to save the tiger as, on the endangered species list, all sub-species of tigers are considered critically endangered species.

The tiger, one of the most magnificent animals in the world, is also one of the most endangered species in the world. A cat of beauty, strength and majesty; the tiger is master of all and subject to none – except humans.

www.tigersincrisis.com

EXERCISE 4.2

Complete a table like this by copying sentences or phrases in each column.

Factual language	Emotive language

Build detail in sentences

Look at this sentence from the article about tigers:

The tiger, one of the most magnificent animals in the world, is also one of the most endangered species in the world.

The author has inserted a phrase which gives more detail and more persuasive force:

Main sentence	Detailed sentence
The tiger is also one of the most endangered species in the world.	The tiger, **one of the most magnificent animals in the world**, is also one of the most endangered species in the world.

EXERCISE 4.3

Try adding detail to these sentences.

1 The orang-utan, ________________, is endangered.

2 Large areas of rainforest, ________________, are being lost to deforestation.

3 Many of the world's rivers, ________________, are becoming polluted.

Using and ordering complex sentences

Compare these two sentences:

Many tigers are killed every year because their body parts are used in traditional medicines.

Because their body parts are used in traditional medicines, many tigers are killed every year.

These are two versions of the same complex sentence.

There is a main clause and a subordinate clause.

many tigers are killed every year	because their body parts are used in traditional medicines

The word *because* is the conjunction that links the subordinate clause to the main clause.

A complex sentence can be written in either order:

- main clause → subordinate clause
- subordinate clause → main clause

EXERCISE 4.4

Match a main clause and a subordinate clause from each list.

Try writing the sentence in different orders and judge the different effects.

Main clause	Subordinate clause
tigers prefer to live in dense vegetation	although some people think there are even fewer
researchers find it difficult to track tigers	so they can hide amongst the tall plants
scientists estimate there are only 20 South China tigers in the wild	because their territory covers many miles

GLOSSARY

arboreal – of trees or woodland
fashion – create or make
foliage – leaves
solitary – alone or only

WORD ATTACK SKILLS

Work out the meaning of the following words as used in the article. How have the prefixes and suffixes changed the meaning of the words?

✔ indigenous
✔ terrestrial
✔ deforestation
✔ insatiable
✔ extinction

LET'S TALK

Work in a small group and think about the following questions:

■ Does the article persuade you that palm oil is problematic?

■ Does it persuade you to want to do more to save orang-utans?

■ What could be said for and against the arguments put forward here?

Work together to collect ideas for both sides of the argument, then hold a class debate.

Identifying bias, opinion and fact

What We Do **News** **Facts** **Help Us** **About**

Save the orang-utan

About the orang-utan

▲ Orang-utan means People of the Forest

Orang-utans are a species of great ape found only in South East Asia on the islands of Borneo and Sumatra, although evidence of their existence has been found in Java, Vietnam and China. The gentle red ape demonstrates significant intelligence, with an ability to reason and think and is one of our closest relatives, sharing 97 per cent of the same DNA as humans.

Indigenous peoples of Indonesia and Malaysia call this ape 'Orang Hutan' literally translating into English as People of the Forest. In times past, the people of the jungle would not kill them because they felt the orang-utan was simply a person hiding in the trees, trying to avoid having to go to work or become a slave.

Orang-utans are unique in the ape world. There are four kinds of great apes: gorillas, chimpanzees, bonobos and orang-utans. Only the orang-utan comes from Asia; the others all come from Africa. There are two separate species of orang-utan – the Sumatran orang-utan (*Pongo abelii*) and the Bornean orang-utan (*Pongo pygmaeus*). Orang-utans are only found on the islands of Sumatra and Borneo.

The orang-utan is the only strictly **arboreal** ape and is actually the largest tree living mammal in the world. The rest of the apes do climb and build sleeping nests in the trees, but are primarily terrestrial (spending their lives on the ground). Every night they **fashion** nests, in which they sleep, from branches and **foliage**. They are more **solitary** than the other apes, with males and females generally coming together only to mate. Even the hair colour of the orang-utan, a bright reddish brown, is unique in the ape world.

The devastating effect of palm oil

Orang-utans are being pushed to the brink. In the past decade alone, their numbers have fallen by up to half.

Probably the biggest threat is the loss of their natural habitat – due to industrial scale deforestation, forest fires, mining interests and conversion to palm oil plantations. **In the past 20 years, around 80% of suitable orang-utan habitat has disappeared.** And only a tiny 2% of what remains is legally protected.

The world's insatiable demand for palm oil is one major factor in the orang-utan's decline. And it is estimated that palm oil is present in more than half of the packaged supermarket products on sale in the UK today.

Grown sustainably, palm oil can provide vital livelihoods in an environmentally friendly way. But so far, too many manufacturers seem reluctant to pay the little extra for sustainably produced oil.

The huge demand is placing an unbearable strain on the remaining rainforests of the world – not least in Borneo. And, as the forests disappear, the orang-utan inches closer and closer to extinction.

Please help us act now to avoid disaster. The orang-utan **can** be saved.

https://savetheorangutan.org/

Reading

Reading for factual information

EXERCISE 4.5

1 From the first section of the extract, with the heading 'About the orang-utan', write down five facts that you have learned about the orang-utan.

2 Find two details that make orang-utans 'unique in the ape world'.

3 Explain what is meant by 'arboreal ape'.

4 Using your own words, explain what has caused the numbers of the orang-utan to decline. Why in particular is the worldwide demand for palm oil causing so much of a problem?

Reading for bias and opinion

EXERCISE 4.6

1 Put this sentence into your own words: 'Grown sustainably, palm oil can provide vital livelihoods in an environmentally friendly way.'

2 Find five words in the extract that are used to persuade the reader. Explain how they add persuasive force.

3 Find and copy a sentence that contains bias. Underline the word or words that have the purpose of persuasion in the sentence.

Key skills

Using modal adverbs in persuasive language

Find the sentence in the extract about orang-utans beginning:

Probably the biggest threat is...

The word *probably* is a modal adverb.

Here are some more modal adverbs:

- certainly
- surely
- possibly
- without doubt
- indubitably
- perhaps
- maybe

They can be used at the beginning of a sentence:
- **Certainly**, the orang-utan is one of our nearest relatives.
- **Without doubt**, we must do something to save them.
- **Possibly**, they could soon be extinct.

Modal adverbs can also appear before the main verb.
- We **really** must prevent deforestation.
- In ten years, the orang-utan will **surely** be extinct.

EXERCISE 4.7
Use modal adverbs to add persuasive force to five sentences about environmental issues.

Speaking and listening

Seeing both sides of an argument

There are many important environmental issues, including:

- climate change
- extinctions
- animal welfare
- pollution.

Many people have strong opinions about some of these issues.

> We must stop chopping down rainforests.

> We should protect animals more than humans.

> Single-use plastics should be banned.

> There are more important issues than climate change.

EXERCISE 4.8

You may already agree or disagree with some of these statements. Spend some quiet reflection deciding for yourself on whether you agree or disagree strongly with any of these statements.

Now write down your reasons for agreeing or disagreeing. You only need to make notes at this stage.

Reasons I agree:
- flooding
- damage to wildlife

Prepare for a class debate

As a class, choose a statement to debate. You could choose one of the speech bubbles from page **66**, or think of your own.

Your teacher will put you into one of two groups: A or B.
Group A will have to argue for the statement.
Group B will argue against the statement.

LET'S TALK

Work with someone else who is in your group.

Spend some time thinking of arguments that could support your group's point of view.

You do not have to agree personally. The point is to think of the reasons, facts and beliefs that are related to the idea.

HINT

You may be asked to argue against what you actually believe. Do not worry: this is an important skill.
It will help you to see both sides of the argument.

Activity 4.7

Write a short paragraph that argues for your group's point of view. Include:
- facts and opinions
- modal adverbs
- modal verbs.

Debate time!

Now it is time for the class debate: group A and group B should each deliver their arguments, taking it in turns.

When you are listening to the other group, take notes.

When the arguments have all been read out, spend some time debating the ideas further.

HINT

When you listen, you may not always agree with what you hear.

If you disagree, you should use polite language, such as 'You made a good point. However, in my opinion …'.

Listen carefully and save any questions until an appropriate time.

Writing

Activity 4.8

Working in a small group of three or four, decide on an issue that you all consider to be of importance to your country in today's world and produce a web-based campaign intended to educate (that is, to inform) people of your age in other countries about the issue.

The campaign should also encourage them to care about the issue and to join you to promote it. The extract from the Tigers in Crisis website, printed on page 62, may give you some ideas on the tone and mood for your website campaign but you don't have to take endangered animals as your subject!

Design and write a cover page, an 'About us' page and include one advertisement to persuade people to take action.

> **HINT**
>
> As this is a group activity, it would be a good idea for each member of the group to proofread and to suggest changes and improvement to one another's work before the complete campaign is published.

EXERCISE 4.9

Each person in your group is going to write a news article to be published on your website.

Remind yourself of the features of non-fiction texts and think about which ones you should use to make your campaign effective. For example:
- headings
- sub-headings
- quotes
- photographs
- diagrams

Remember to use language precisely to make clear your intended purpose to your readers and to structure and sequence what you write to emphasise your overall message to your readers. You should also think about using a variety of layouts and textual features to attract readers to key points of your campaign.

Follow the steps in the writing cycle on page v to plan, draft, edit, proofread and present your web article.

> **HINT**
>
> In your own writing, you should try to vary the types of sentences you use to give variety to your expression – too many simple sentences soon become monotonous. As a general rule, the more complicated your ideas are, the more likely you are to use lengthy sentences.

Speaking and listening

Activity 4.9

Shoot a five-minute video for your website. The video is the 'hook' to get people interested in your campaign. The less you say, the more people will remember. Mention the problem, the solution, how the campaign works and the call to action.

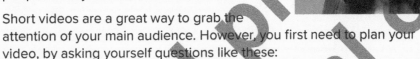

A well-written and performed script is the key to a successful video for a website. It is a quick and simple way to tell your story and to tell people what you want them to do next.

Short videos are a great way to grab the attention of your main audience. However, you first need to plan your video, by asking yourself questions like these:

- Who is the main audience?
- What do we want to tell them about the problem and the solution?
- What tone will we set (emotional, funny, serious)?
- What do we want them to do next (the call to action)?

You will need to write a draft script and revise it until you are satisfied with it. Then, draw a storyboard for your video. All group members will be part of this video. Present the content of the video as a group performance to the rest of your class.

Remember to consider all features of communication:
- your non-verbal communication such as body language and facial expression
- your words, including their tone and register
- the message: what you are trying to communicate and the emotive and persuasive language you will need to persuade people to action
- visual aids, props and other ways to get and keep people's attention.

Activity 4.10

Evaluate your own website, then those of other groups.

Remember to take turns in your groups and assign roles to report back to the class.
- What did you do well? What could you (or other groups) have done better?
- Did the website communicate its purpose?
- Did it use text and visuals well?
- Was its message clear?
- Did it use emotive and persuasive language?
- Was the writing clear, grammatically correct, free of spelling errors or typing mistakes?

Writing

Formal or business letters

One occasion in our everyday lives when we may have to write to inform is when we need to write a letter to an organisation or a business. Letters of this type are known as formal or business letters and there is a standard form in which they should be set out.

A formal letter should be set out like this:

> The title and address of the person to whom you are sending the letter then goes on the left-hand side of the page.

> Add the current date.

> Write the salutation (such as 'Dear Sir/Madam') directly under the date.

> Finish your letter with either 'Yours sincerely' (if you have named the person you are writing to) or 'Yours faithfully' or 'Yours truly'.

> Write your own address at the top right-hand side of the page.

> If it is necessary to quote a reference or say what subject your letter is about, this should be placed on the following line.

> Say why you are writing the letter. Give some background and make a request or a comment. Do this in two or three short paragraphs.

> Sign off the letter with both your first and family name.

Blk A–B
East Kalimantan
Borneo

Marie Sigvardt
Head of Programmes
Save the Orang-utan
Borneo
12 June 2021

Dear Ms Sigvart

Re: Application to be a volunteer in the programme

I have seen the amazing rehabilitation programmes that you do with orang-utans. I would really like to volunteer my services during this school holiday. I love animals and already volunteer at the local animal shelter. I am enthusiastic and I work very hard. I have read all the books I can find in our school library about orang-utans.

Could you please give me more information about how to apply for this programme? I would relish the opportunity to look after baby orang-utans and teach them how to climb, build shelters and forage for food.

Yours sincerely

James Reddy

EXERCISE 4.10

Write a formal letter to a local charity or animal organisation to ask how you can volunteer for the sanctuary or offer help.

Writing

Applying your language skills

You have learned:

- to identify bias and use emotive language
- to use modal verbs and adverbs to add persuasive force
- to build detail into complex sentences
- to express a personal viewpoint.

EXERCISE 4.11

Plan and write a formal letter about an issue to argue for change.
The purpose is to argue for change that can be achieved through local action.

You could choose an issue from:
- recycling
- protecting woodland
- animal welfare
- plastics.

Here are some ideas.

> I will ask my headteacher to ban plastic water bottles.

> I will write to my local government to demand an end to pollution.

> I will write to a global food company to demand they protect forests by not using palm oil.

Your goal is to write a formal letter that is persuasive and uses the language skills you have learned so far.

Follow this planning model:
Step 1: Plan by making notes of the main arguments.
Step 2: Write a first draft.
Step 3: Share with a partner. Check each other's work for accuracy.
Step 4: Write an improved draft.

Reviewing

Reflect on the non-fiction texts you've read in this chapter

Talk about:

- which texts you liked and which you didn't like
- which you think were well-written and why
- what techniques the writers used to create effects in their writing
- what texts you have read that are similar to these.

If you like reading non-fiction, try these books:

- *Whale Quest: Working together to Save Endangered Species* by Karen Romano Young
- *This Book Will (Help) Cool the Climate* by Isabel Thomas
- *Earth Heroes: Twenty Inspiring Stories of People Saving Our World* by Lily Dyu
- *World Without Fish* by Mark Kurlansky
- *Endangered Wildlife: Rescuing Mammals* by Anita Ganeri
- *Eco Stories for Those Who Dare to Care* by Ben Hubbard
- *No One is Too Small to Make a Difference* by Greta Thunberg

Talk about the great new skills you have learned.

Reflect on your learning in this chapter

- What new skills and techniques have you learned to improve your reading, listening and speaking and writing?
- Make a list of things you would like to practise further.
  - Compile a plan for tackling these.
  - Discuss your lists and ideas with a partner and your teacher.

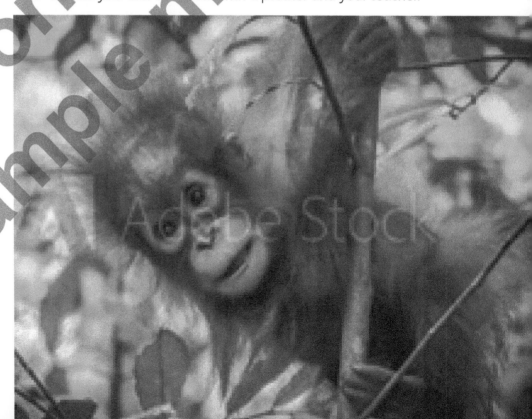

5 It's tradition!

Reading
★ Folk tales
★ Ballads

Speaking and listening
★ Listening to a folk tale
★ Retelling traditional tales
★ Listening to a ballad
★ Delivering a presentation on an interesting person

IT'S TRADITION!

Writing
★ A folk tale
★ Using direct speech in your writing

Key skills
★ Revise hyphens and compound sentences
★ Rhythm

LET'S TALK
- Which folk tales do you know?
- How were folk tales passed down through generations? What features made them easy to pass down this way?
- How do folk tales differ from short stories or novels?
- What makes a good storyteller?

Reading

Folk tales

> **Activity 5.1**

1   Work in a group. Tell your group your favourite (or least favourite) folk tale. Briefly say what the folk tale is about and why you like it or don't like it.
2   Skim-read the following extract and discuss what it is about.

KEY WORDS

folk tales stories that are handed down from generation to generation, usually in spoken form

genre a particular type of literature or other art form, e.g. novel, poetry, science fiction

oral storytelling a story in spoken form

onomatopoeia when the sound of a word echoes its meaning, e.g. *boom*

Extract: 'Traditional folk tales'

How old are folk tales?

Folk tales are one of the earliest **genres** of story-telling. Many of them were originally made up centuries ago before writing and printing were in common use. The stories were handed down from generation to generation, usually in spoken form. Over the years, the different tellers of the original stories added their own details and adapted the stories to their particular listeners. Eventually, many of these traditional stories were collected into books by folklorists (people who study the traditions and culture of the past) and preserved for future readers. In some parts of the world, the tradition of **oral storytelling** continues today. Some stories are long forgotten but many stories have survived.

Nature

Many folk tales use nature to tell a story, for example, about the relationship between humans and nature, or people's negative or positive behaviour towards nature, or to try to explain natural phenomena (like why the moon is in the sky or why a leopard has spots).

Morals and lessons

Many of the original folk tales contain a moral or a lesson and many of these early stories form the basis of the plots of more sophisticated stories and novels nowadays. Folklorists have found that many of the basic plots are common to more than one culture and can be found in the tales of countries from different continents.

They use characters that the audience can easily relate to who are either good or bad. Very often the characters are animals. They usually end with good triumphing over evil.

Oral tradition

A story that is told orally is spoken out loud. Stories that are part of the oral tradition usually contain quite a lot of repeated details and vocabulary. This is a deliberate attempt on the storyteller's part to make sure that the listeners can remember what has happened as they do not have printed copies of the story in which they can turn back a few pages to check details. These stories often use dialogue (direct speech) as well as literary devices such as **onomatopoeia**, similes and metaphors to keep the attention of listeners.

Listening

Spotlight on: listening

We listen to stories for enjoyment and to learn about different cultures and ideas. When you listen to a story there are no visual clues to help you understand. You need to concentrate on what you hear.

■ Listen for key words.

■ Try to picture what is happening as you listen.

■ Make notes of things you don't understand or write short questions to answer when you listen to the story again.

EXERCISE 5.1

1 Listen to the first part of a folk tale called 'Stripes Tiger and the Boy'. As you listen, make notes or questions about the content. For example: *Who is Rahul? Where is he? What's the tiger's name?*

2 Listen to the folk tale again and answer your own questions.

Activity 5.2

In a pair, quickly discuss and summarise what has happened in the folk tale so far. What do you think may happen next?

Talk about the features of this folk tale.

■ How does it begin?

■ Who are the main characters?

■ Do you think this tale has a moral lesson?

3 Then read this summary of the next part of the story:

> The tiger agreed to give Rahul two more chances. They met a horse called Miss Mare and asked her opinion. The horse agreed that humans were cruel. She said that Stripes should eat Rahul. Then they met a young girl called Preety. She asked to see the cage from which Stripes had been set free …

You will read the rest of the story.

Reading and speaking

WORD ATTACK SKILLS

Work out the meaning of the following words and expressions:

✔ exasperated
✔ gnashing
✔ head or tail
✔ reluctantly
✔ ungrateful

Spotlight on: reading aloud

■ Try to read ahead so that you can plan for direct speech or voices.
■ Read loud enough so that the class can hear you.
■ Use the punctuation to guide your pauses: a short pause for a comma or a dash, and a longer one for a full stop.
■ Try to use voices and different speech patterns for the different characters.
■ Look up occasionally to make eye contact with your audience (the class).

EXERCISE 5.2

Your teacher will ask you to read a section of this folk tale aloud.

Extract: 'Stripes Tiger and the Boy'

'But how can I tell you when I haven't seen a cage around? I can't understand what the two of you are talking about at all!' said Preety.

'We are talking about the cage I was in,' explained an **exasperated** Stripes. 'You see __'

'Exactly, I don't see at all,' said Preety, very sweetly. 'How can you "set him free", when he is already free?'

She turned towards Stripes. 'And how did you get into a cage, I want to know.'

'Grr,' said Stripes, **gnashing** his teeth. These humans are really dumb. He counted to 10 to avoid losing his temper. And then he began to explain.

'Last night I had come to the village to steal a lamb when I fell into a trap prepared by the villagers. They put me in a cage. This fool ...'

'Oh! What sort of cage was it and where was it?' interrupted Preety. 'I can't make **head or tail** of what you say.'

'A large strong wooden cage,' said Rahul.

'See here, I can't tell you without getting an idea of the cage,' said Preety. 'Why don't you two show me the cage? I will then give an answer in a second.' And so saying she winked at Stripes.

Stripes was love struck. Joyfully he took her small hand in his large paw and danced down the road towards the cage.

The unfortunate Rahul dragged his heels **reluctantly**.

At the cage Preety took over. 'Here Rahul, let's start at the beginning. Show me where you stood and where Mr Stripes was when you came along.'

'I was coming down this little path,' said Rahul.

'And Mr Stripes, you?' asked Preety.

'Here, inside the cage, of course,' replied Stripes.

'Oh, I would think this cage is not big enough for you, Mr Stripes. Won't you show me how you managed to stay in with your huge body?' asked Preety with an innocent look.

'See, I can get in and I was sitting here,' so saying Stripes leapt into the cage.

'Ahh! So that's where you were. But your paws can reach out. Why didn't you come out yourself?' asked Preety.

'I couldn't as the door was locked,' growled Stripes feeling quite uneasy at being back in the cage.

'Oh, excuse me,' said Preety looking suitably stupid. 'Being human I am very stupid. I can't imagine until you show me how. Will you show me how it works?'

Rahul pushed the door in. 'Like this.'

'And the lock?' asked Preety. 'Where is it?'

'Here!' cried Rahul. And he shut and bolted the door!

'Aha! So that's it,' said Preety clapping her hands. 'It does lock the door tightly.

'And now Rahul, as the door is locked, I suggest it stays locked. As for you, Mr Stripes, you have been very wicked and *ungrateful*. I hope you are locked up for a very long time.' Saying this, Preety took Rahul's arm and led him away.

B. Sumangal

LET'S TALK

Talk about the key features of folk tales that you have noticed in the folk tale 'Stripes Tiger and the Boy'. Look at what you read on page 74 about this.

EXTENSION

Act out the story in a small group. Think about how you should use your voice and what gestures and movements will help convey your character.

HINT

Remember how Preety tricks the Tiger by asking questions.

EXERCISE 5.3

1 Why had the villagers put Stripes into a cage?

2 Explain why Mr Bray and Miss Mare did not care for humans.

3 Explained how Preety tricked Stripes back into the cage.

4 Describe Rahul's character and behaviour as fully as you can. Do you think he was wrong to let Stripes out of the cage in the first place?

5 Does this folk tale have a lesson or a moral? If so, what is it?

Spelling

1 Read these words from the folk tale aloud. What do you need to remember when you write these words: *dumb, two, know, tightly*?

2 Write a sentence using each word in question 1.

3 Explain the spelling rule in:
   ■ sitting
   ■ dragged.

4 Complete the following sentences and apply the rule you identified in question 3.
   a As I was (get) up, the Tiger pounced on me.
   b 'Why are you (put) the tiger in the cage?' the man asked.

Reading

Author: Rohini Chowdhury

Rohini Chowdhury (born in 1950) is a children's writer and illustrator in India. She writes in Hindi and English.

Activity 5.3

Work in a pair. Discuss what reading strategies you can use for longer extracts, like the one below, such as making notes or creating a mind map.

Extract: 'Why the Sky is So High'

WORD ATTACK SKILLS

1 Work out the meaning of the following words:
  ✔ plied
  ✔ thwacked
2 Give another word for a person who lives alone and keeps away from other people.

Long ago, the Sky was quite low. If you stood on a stool and stretched your hands up as high as they would go, you could touch the Sky.

At that time, far on the Horizon, where the Sky was always especially low, there was a village. In that village, in a little mud hut thatched with straw, there lived a bent Old Woman.

This bent Old Woman was the oldest woman in that village, possibly the oldest woman in the world. She was so old she no longer remembered any other way of being. She lived all alone in her little mud hut, for she had neither friend nor family left in this world. She had nowhere to go and no one to talk to. So all day long, she would potter round her hut, first cleaning this corner, now dusting that, now scrubbing this bit of floor, now sweeping that. The bent Old Woman thought of nothing else any more, except more and more ways of sweeping and scrubbing her little mud hut.

One hot summer, the land was dry with thirst. There was dust everywhere – on the trees, on the roofs of huts and houses, in people's throats and eyes, even in the air. All over the village people were coughing and sneezing and choking with the dust. Even the poor old Sky was not spared – it was so close to the ground that the slightest bit of wind would set it coughing with the dust that rose from the parched land.

The bent Old Woman's hut too was covered with dust. The Old Woman swept and swept and swept the little hut with her broom. She swept the inside of her hut, she swept the outside of her hut, she swept the front step and she swept the front yard. But the dust rose all around her in great brown clouds – the more she swept and **plied** her broom, the more the dust that rose from the earth.

The poor Sky began to choke with all the dust that the bent Old Woman was raising with her broom. The dust got into its throat and tickled its nose and made it sneeze – a great big sneeze that shook the world with its thunder. People covered their heads and ran indoors in fright. But the bent Old Woman barely noticed – she kept on sweeping with her broom.

The Sky sneezed again – the dust was becoming unbearable. It got into its eyes and made them water – so that great heavy drops of rain began falling into the dry dust below. The bent Old Woman barely noticed – till finally a big splodgy raindrop fell right on to the patch she had just swept.

The bent Old Woman glared at the Sky and scrubbed the splodgy raindrop away. But then another raindrop fell, and another, till her swept and scrubbed front step was blotchy with raindrops.

This was more than the bent Old Woman could bear. She stood up as straight as she could with her bent old back and shook her fist at the Sky yelling at it to stop raining on her nice clean front step. She cursed the Sky and threatened it, but the poor old Sky couldn't stop raining – its eyes were still so full of dust with all her sweeping.

At last, the bent Old Woman was so angry, that she picked up her broom, and **thwacked** the Sky with it.

The Sky gave another great sneeze and jumped out of her way. But the bent Old Woman kept thwacking it with her broom, again and again and again.

Finally the Sky could take it no more – the dust, the Old Woman's cursing, and especially her broom, thwacking it again and again and again. Sneezing and coughing, thundering and raining, the Sky flew up, up and away – out of reach of the Old Woman's broom and swore never to come down again.

So that is why the Sky is so high. Even on the Horizon, where it seems to be touching the earth, it really isn't any more.

Retold by Rohini Chowdhury

LET'S TALK

What does this folk tale try to explain? How is it different from the folk tale on pages 75–77?

EXERCISE 5.4

2 Give three details about the Old Woman and the life she led.
3 Why was there so much dust?
4 What problems did the dust cause and how did the Sky react?
5 In your own words, describe how the Old Woman acyed towards the Sky.
6 According to the story, why is the Sky so high?

Read this extract from 'Why the Sky is So High', in which the author has used several dashes. Discuss the effect of these dashes.

HINT

Remember that dashes can give more emphasis to words or phrases in a sentence. They can also introduce an opinion or an explanation.

> People covered their heads and ran indoors in fright. But the bent Old Woman barely noticed – she kept on sweeping with her broom. The Sky sneezed again – the dust was becoming unbearable. It got into its eyes and made them water – so that great heavy drops of rain began falling into the dry dust below. The bent Old Woman barely noticed – till finally a big splodgy raindrop fell right on to the patch she had just swept.

Reading and speaking

In this folk tale from Tibet, panic is caused in the forest when the rabbits mistakenly believe that Plop is coming. The misunderstanding is only discovered later, when the lion does not panic.

> **LET'S TALK**
>
> This story you are going to read and discuss is similar to European stories such as Chicken Licken, in which a chicken believes that the sky is falling and the world is coming to an end.
>
> 1   Talk about or retell the Chicken Licken in your group if you know the story. Ask your teacher or look it up online if you do not know it.
> 2   Why do you think that similar stories exist in many different cultures?

Spotlight on: setting

The story is set in Tibet. What clues are there in the text?

Extract: 'Plop!'

Many, many years ago there were six rabbits who lived on the shore of a lake, in a forest. One fine day, a big ripe fruit on one of the biggest trees fell down into the lake, making a loud 'plop!' when it hit the water. The rabbits were terrified, not knowing what this noise could be, and at once made off as fast as their four legs could carry them.

A fox saw them fleeing and called out, 'Why are you flying?'

The rabbits said, 'Plop is coming!'

When the fox heard this, he immediately started to flee with them. Next they ran into a monkey, who queried, 'Why are you in such a hurry?'

'Plop is coming!' replied the fox. So the monkey also joined in their flight.

Thus the news spread from mouth to mouth until a deer, a pig, a buffalo, a rhinoceros, an elephant, a black bear, a brown bear, a leopard, a tiger, and a lion were all running away, helter-skelter.

WORD ATTACK SKILLS

Look up the word *naught*. It is an Old English word. What does it mean? Suggest other words with the same spelling pattern or which sound the same.

LET'S TALK

What is the moral or lesson in this story?

They had no thought at all, except to fly. The faster they ran, the more frightened they became.

At the foot of the hill there lived a lion with a great long mane. When he caught sight of the other lion running, he roared to him, 'Brother, you have claws and teeth, and you are the strongest of all animals. Why are you running like mad?'

'Plop is coming!' the running lion panted.

'Who's Plop? Where is he?' the lion with the long mane demanded.

'Well, I don't really know,' he faltered.

'Why make such a fuss then?' the long-maned lion went on. 'Let's find out what it is first. Who told you about it?'

'The tiger told me.'

The inquisitive lion with the long mane asked the tiger, who said that the leopard had told him, so the lion turned to the leopard, and the leopard answered that he had heard it from the brown bear. The question was passed on to the brown bear, who said he had heard it from the black bear. In this way, the black bear, the elephant, the rhinoceros, the buffalo, the pig, and the deer were all asked, one by one, and each of them said he was told by someone else.

Finally it came down to the fox's testimony, and he said, 'The rabbits told me.'

Then the lion went up to the rabbits, who squeaked in chorus, 'All six of us heard this terrible plop with our own ears. Come with us, we'll show you where we heard him.'

They led him to the forest, and pointing at it, they told the lion, 'The terrible plop is there.'

Just at this moment another big fruit fell from the tree and dropped into the water with a deep 'plop!'

The lion sneered.

'Now, look, all of you!' he said. 'You've all seen what that plop is. It's only the sound of a fruit dropping into the water. What is so terrifying about that? You almost ran your legs off!'

They breathed a sigh of relief. The panic was all for **naught**.

Activity 5.5

Talk about these questions in your group and then give feedback to the class. Remember to give each person an opportunity to speak.

1 What features of folk tales (repetition, etc.) do you find in these stories? How far do you think they help readers to engage with the stories? (Note that the two stories use repetition in slightly different ways.)

2 Explain how animals or nature are used in the two extracts to tell the story. Why are they used?

Writing and speaking

Activity 5.6

Work in pairs. Create compound adjectives with hyphens using the underlined words in these sentences. Then use your compound words and rewrite each sentence. Share and discuss your sentences with another pair.

1 The house was owned by a woman <u>who was 100 years old</u>.
2 She made a decision <u>at the last minute</u> to buy a new book.
3 That is a treat <u>that makes my mouth water</u>.
4 This folk tale is a story <u>that was forgotten for a long time</u>.

HINT
You learned about how dashes can be used for emphasis in Chapter 1. A dash can also be used as a **stylistic device**, particularly in direct speech, to suggest the nature of a character in a work of fiction.

Direct speech is an effective way of allowing the reader to hear the voices of the characters in a written story. Direct speech brings a story to life and helps the reader understand the characters and their personalities.

Remember to use the correct punctuation.
- Use speech marks (inverted commas) to show the beginning and then end of the spoken words.
- Use a comma before the words that are spoken.
- Start a new line for each speaker.

EXERCISE 5.5
Read the beginning of this extract from the story 'Plop!'. Then use direct speech with the correct punctuation to make this section more lively. You can rewrite the section that is not already in direct speech. You can change the text a little but keep the same meaning.

'Why make such a fuss then?' the long-maned lion went on. 'Let's find out what it is first. Who told you about it?'

'The tiger told me.'

The inquisitive lion with the long mane asked the tiger, who said that the leopard had told him, so the lion turned to the leopard, and the leopard answered that he had heard it from the brown bear. The question was passed on to the brown bear, who said he had heard it from the black bear. In this way, the black bear, the elephant, the rhinoceros, the buffalo, the pig, and the deer were all asked, one by one, and each of them said he was told by someone else.

Key skills

Revise hyphens

We use hyphens to create compound words that are shorter and more powerful than longer descriptions. Look at these examples:

... the <u>long-maned</u> lion ran on.

This is a compound adjective that is used instead of 'the lion with the long mane'.

... a <u>dust-covered</u> house

This is a compound adjective that is used instead of 'the house is covered in dust'.

Note: not all compound words have hyphens. The word 'storyteller' is an example of a compound word for which we do not use a hyphen.

Revise compound sentences

Writers use compound sentences to add detail to what they are writing.

Activity 5.7

Look at the compound sentences below from the folk tales you have read. Find the clauses by identifying the verbs. Then discuss how the clauses are linked.

1 'Brother, you have claws and teeth, and you are the strongest of all animals.'
2 Just at this moment another big fruit fell from the tree and dropped into the water with a deep 'plop!'
3 But the bent Old Woman barely noticed – she kept on sweeping with her broom.
4 She swept the inside of her hut, she swept the outside of her hut, she swept the front step and she swept the front yard.

EXERCISE 5.6

Make compound sentences. Add detail to the following sentences by adding another main (independent) clause. Link the clauses in the sentences with a connective or a punctuation mark.

1 'I kill prey for my food,' snarled the tiger.
2 The Old Woman glared at the Sky.
3 The rabbits heard a loud 'plop'.
4 She has read many folk tales about tigers.
5 It was raining quite hard.

Listening and reading

Ballads

Ballads are poems that tell stories. Like folk takes, many ballads were first composed hundreds of years ago by people whom we don't know. They were passed down through the generations in song before they were written down later.

Ballads often use repetition, direct speech and literary devices such as **alliteration** and onomatopoeia to get the attention of listeners and readers. Ballads are written in rhyming verse, often in stanzas of four lines each.

KEY WORDS
alliteration the repetition of consonant sounds at the beginning of words

Activity 5.8

1 Listen to the ballad 'The Bold Pedlar and Robin Hood'. Write down the main sequence of events in the ballad.
2 Read the ballad and confirm that you understand the gist of the story. Discuss this with a group or partner.
3 Look for clues about the setting and historical context of the ballad as you listen and read.

WORD ATTACK SKILLS

Work out the meaning for the following words or phrases.
- ✔ trudged
- ✔ gay
- ✔ bowstrings
- ✔ perch
- ✔ thrash
- ✔ sheathed their swords

'The Bold Pedlar and Robin Hood'

This tis one of many ballads that tell of events in the life of the legendary outlaw Robin Hood. In this story, Robin and one of his Merry Men, little John (so-called because he was very large in size), meet a pedlar (a travelling salesperson). At first it looks as if the two outlaws are planning to rob the pedlar, but the story takes an unexpected twist.

There chanced to be a Pedlar bold,
A Pedlar bold there chanced to be;
He put his pack all on his back,
And so merrily trudged over the lear.

By chance he met two troublesome men,
Two troublesome men they chanced to be,
The one of them was bold Robin Hood,
And the other was little John so free.

O Pedlar, Pedlar, what is in thy pack?
Come speedily and tell to me.
I've several suits of the gay green silks,
And silken bowstrings by two or three.

If you have several suits of the gay green silk,
And silken bowstrings two or three
Then, by my body, cries little John,
One half of your pack shall belong to me.

O nay, O nay, said the pedlar bold,
O nay, O nay, that can never be
For there's never a man from fair Nottingham,
Can take one half my pack from me.

Then the Pedlar he pulled off his pack,
And put it a little below his knee,
Saying, If you do move me one perch from this,
My pack and all shall gang with thee.

Then little John he drew his sword,

▲ Robin Hood and his Merry Men

The Pedlar by his pack did stand,

They fought until they both did sweat,

Till he cried, Pedlar, pray hold your hand.

Then Robin Hood he was standing by,

And he did laugh most heartily,

Saying, I could find a man of smaller scale,

Could thrash the Pedlar and also thee.

Go you try, master, says little John,

Go you try, master, most speedily,

For by my body, says little John,

I am sure this night you will know me.

Then Robin Hood he drew his sword,

And the pedlar by his pack did stand;

They fought till the blood in streams did flow,

Till he cried, Pedlar, pray hold your hand.

O Pedlar, Pedlar, what is thy name?

Come speedily and tell to me.

Come, my name I ne'er will tell,

Till both your names you have told to me.

The one of us is bold Robin Hood,

And the other is little John so free.

Now, says the Pedlar, it lays to my good will,

Whether my name I choose to tell to thee.

I am Gamble Gold of the gay green woods,

And I travelled far beyond the sea,

For killing a man in my father's land,

And from my country was forced to flee.

If you are Gamble Gold of the gay green woods,

And travelled far beyond the sea,

You are my mother's own sister's son,

What nearer cousins can we be?

They sheathed their swords, with friendly words,

So merrily they did agree,

They went to a tavern and there they dined,

And cracked bottles most merrily.

Anonymous

> **1** What do you think is going to happen?

> **2** Why does Robin only ask for the pedlar's name now? How does it add to the tension in the ballad?

> **3** Why did the poet not say 'aunt's son' rather than 'my mother's own sister's son'? Why are these words used instead?

Activity 5.9

Discuss some of the features of this ballad.

1 Look at the two pairs of underlined phrases on the previous page. Explain what the poet is doing here. What is the effect of this?

2 Find further examples of repetition in the ballad and talk about the effect it has.

3 Find an example of alliteration in the ballad. What effect does this have? (Think about the rhythm.)

4 Find examples of direct speech in the ballad. Identify the speaker and

LONG PAGE

Listening and reading

Many songwriters and poets still use the ballad form today as a way of telling a story through music.

Activity 5.10

You are going to listen to and read an example of a ballad from the twentieth century: it tells the story of another famous outlaw, Pretty Boy Floyd, who was an American bank robber of the 1930s. This time was known as the Great Depression.

Work in a group and do some research on the Great Depression so that you understand the historical context of this extract. Discuss what happened and what effect the Great Depression had on the lives of people in the USA.

EXERCISE 5.7

1 Listen to *The Ballad of Pretty Boy Floyd*. Listen to the rhythm (beat). Write down the main sequence of events.

2 Read the ballad and confirm that you understand the gist of the story. Discuss this with a group or partner.

3 Look for clues about the setting and historical context of the ballad as you listen and read.

About the poet: Woody Guthrie

Woody Guthrie (1912–1967) was an American folk singer and songwriter. He often sang about the hardship of people who were forced to leave their homes.

Spotlight on: audience
Who do you think this text was written for? Do you think the audience would have known who Pretty Boy Floyd was?

'The Ballad of Pretty Boy Floyd'

If you'll gather 'round me, children,
A story I will tell
'Bout Pretty Boy Floyd, an outlaw,
Oklahoma knew him well.

It was in the town of Shawnee,
A Saturday afternoon,
His wife beside him in his wagon
As into town they rode.

There a deputy sheriff approached him
In a manner rather rude,
Vulgar words of anger,
An' his wife she overheard.

Pretty Boy grabbed a log chain,
And the deputy grabbed his gun;
In the fight that followed
He laid that deputy down.

Then he took to the trees and timber
To live a life of shame;

1 What do we call the literary device that repeats the first sound in the following word, such as **g**rabbed ... **g**un; **f**ight ...**f**ollowed; **d**eputy **d**own. What is its effect?

2 Which lines have rhyme? Why is rhyme so popular in ballads?

3 What does the apostrophe before 'bout show? Why is it used here?

4 Why does the poet use direct speech in this verse? What effect does it have?

Every crime in Oklahoma
Was added to his name.

But a many a starving farmer
The same old story told
How the outlaw paid their mortgage
And saved their little homes.

Others tell you 'bout a stranger
That come to beg a meal,
Underneath his napkin
Left a thousand dollar bill.
It was in Oklahoma City,
It was on a Christmas Day,
There was a whole car load of groceries
Come with a note to say:

Well, you say that I'm an outlaw,
You say that I'm a thief.
Here's a Christmas dinner
For the families on relief.

Yes, as through this world I've wandered
I've seen lots of funny men;
Some will rob you with a six-gun,
And some with a fountain pen.

And as through your life you travel,
Yes, as through your life you roam,
You won't never see an outlaw
Drive a family from their home.

Woody Guthrie

Activity 5.11

1 Read one verse of one ballad aloud and clap along to the 'beat' or words that are emphasised. Count how many times you clap on one line. This tells you the rhythm of the ballad.

2 Now read the whole ballad with rhythm. Read the other ballad in the same way.

EXERCISE 5.8

1 Why did Pretty Boy fight the deputy sheriff and what happened as a result of the fight?

2 Read the last two verses carefully. What do you think the writer means by saying that some people will rob you 'with a fountain pen'? How does this comment and what the writer says in the final verse help you to understand the writer's attitude towards Pretty Boy Floyd?

3 Both ballads tell stories of lawbreakers but the writers appear to treat them as heroes rather than villains. How does the writer show bias? Use examples to explain as fully as you can how the writers succeed in presenting the characters as likeable people.

Key skills

 Rhythm

Rhythm is the beat or pace (speed) of a poem. It is formed by the pattern of stressed and unstressed words, for example: You **SAY** that **I'M** a **THIEF**. (The stressed words are in bold. This line has six beats.) Rhythm can strengthen the meaning of words or ideas in a poem.

Spotlight on: using media in a talk

Media such as pictures and notes on a screen or chart can help a speaker to get a message across. They can be a 'hook' that gets the attention of your audience and keeps them interested to the end.

Activity 5.12

After you have heard and given feedback about everyone's talks, have a group discussion to decide which person most deserves to be celebrated.

- Remember to be sensitive to others when taking a turn. Make sure that every person gets an opportunity to speak!
- Identify the points of agreement and disagreement. When you have decided on ONE person, develop an argument to support your choice and defend it against other groups' choices.

Speaking and writing

Making a presentation

When you give a talk, your audience has one chance to understand and be persuaded by the information you are delivering. You need to know who your audience is and make sure that you present information in a way that they will understand and enjoy. To do this you need to plan and you need to decide what media you will use for your presentation.

Keep these questions in mind when you are preparing the presentation.
- Who is my audience?
- What do they want to know about my topic?

Planning a presentation

- Write down your draft ideas.
- Think about how you will support your ideas. Find examples, quotes, pictures or anything that will help to persuade and interest your audience.
- Write a draft with an interesting opening (to introduce your topic) and an effective conclusion (which restates your main ideas).
- Read the draft aloud. You could ask a friend to listen and give you feedback.
- Time yourself. How long does it take? How long is your presentation supposed to be?
- Prepare the media that you have decided to use. You could make a short summary of your main ideas and display them on a screen. You could display photos on paper or on a screen. Remember that everyone needs to be able to see these.
- Then practise!

EXERCISE 5.9

Prepare a talk of 3–4 minutes to give to your class or group, in which you present information about someone (not necessarily famous) whose life deserves to be celebrated in a ballad.
- Explain why you think the person deserves this honour.
- Explain what qualities the ballad should focus on.
- Remember that you need to persuade your audience. Give them reasons to support what you say.

SELF-CHECK

Listen to other learners' talks. Give other learners constructive feedback about their talk, then evaluate your own talk.

CHECKLIST
- Was the talk clear, to the point and interesting?
- Was the talk persuasive?
- Was media used effectively to present and support the talk?
- Was the talk 3–4 minutes long?

You have learned that that folk tales and ballads:

- tell stories about humans and nature
- often have morals or lessons
- were told orally before they were written down
- often include repetition and literary devices to keep the attention of listeners and readers
- can include direct speech to make the characters more real.

HINT

You might like to research some more examples, either from books in libraries or by searching on the internet. As a start, you could look up some of the ballads that have been written about the famous outlaws Robin Hood and Jesse James.

HINT

Remember to do the following:

1 Plan your writing! Refer to the writing cycle on page v.
2 Keep your audience in mind! Are you writing for your peers or for younger children?
3 Think about the different characters, the direct speech and voices they will use. Punctuate your direct speech correctly.

EXERCISE 5.10

Write your own folk tale. You could either make up your own story or write your own version of a traditional story that you have read.

If you write your own story, you could either produce a tale that contains a moral or you could choose to write about something of topical interest, such as an important national or international news story (a major sporting event, for example) or something that has happened closer to home or within your school community.

The choice of subject is up to you. However, it's important to try to include as many of the traditional features of the style of the original tales or ballads as you can to make yours sound authentic.

EXTENSION

In a small group, write your own ballad.

Remember to think about rhyme and rhythm. Repeat words and sentences to help create this. Use alliteration and onomatopoeia too.

Activity 5.13

You have written your own folk tale, which will be part of a small **anthology** (with those of fellow group members). Prepare a group short talk about your anthology. Give it a title and find or draw a picture to illustrate its cover as a visual aid.

Prepare a multimedia presentation (you could include pieces of recorded text from the folk tale or do a slide presentation). Think about which media will work the best for you.

KEY WORD

anthology a published collection of writing, usually of poems or short stories

Reviewing

Reflect on the folk tales and ballads you've read in this chapter

Talk about the texts you engaged with in this chapter.

- Which texts did you like and which didn't you like?
- Which do you think were well-written and why?
- What features did the writers use in their folk tales and ballads?
- What texts have you read that are similar to these?

If you like reading ballads and folk tales, try these books:

- *The Monster Stick and Other Appalachian Tall Tales* by Paul Lepp
- *Norse Mythology* by Neil Gaiman
- The folk tales of the Brothers Grimm

You could also listen to the following ballads:

- 'Dust Bowl Ballads' by Woody Guthrie
- 'A Hard Rain's a-Gonna Fall' by Bob Dylan

Reflect on your learning in this chapter

- What techniques have you learned to improve your reading, listening and speaking and writing? For example, think of how punctuating direct speech correctly can improve your stories and articles.
- How did using compound sentences help you to communicate meaning better?
- How does rhythm affect poetry and songs? With a partner, discuss what you liked about the rhythm in one of the texts you have looked at in this chapter.
- Make a list of things that you would like to practise in your writing more.
  - Compile a plan for tackling these.
  - Discuss your ideas with your classmates and your teacher.

6 Tell me a (short) story

Reading
★ Understanding genres
★ Compound and complex sentences in fiction
★ Reading different settings from different genres

Speaking and listening
★ A speech about your favourite genre
★ Presenting an extract from a book you like

TELL ME A (SHORT) STORY

Writing
★ Using setting to create an effect
★ Revising your own work
★ Writing an episode of a story

Key skills
★ Building detail in simple sentences

LET'S TALK
We read stories for entertainment and enjoyment. Short stories are fiction writing that you'd usually read in one sitting. You have already looked at a popular type of short story in Chapter 5 – folk tales. However, short stories have taken many forms since their invention and are not limited to just older genres such as myths and legends. In this chapter we will explore a range of different short stories.

■ What short stories have you read?

■ Based on the features of a novel or story that you know about, what do you think the features of a short story will be?

■ What makes short stories different to folk tales or novels?

Reading

Genres and main features

Fiction is often sorted into genres. A genre is a category of fiction. Different genres have particular features.

Read the summaries below.

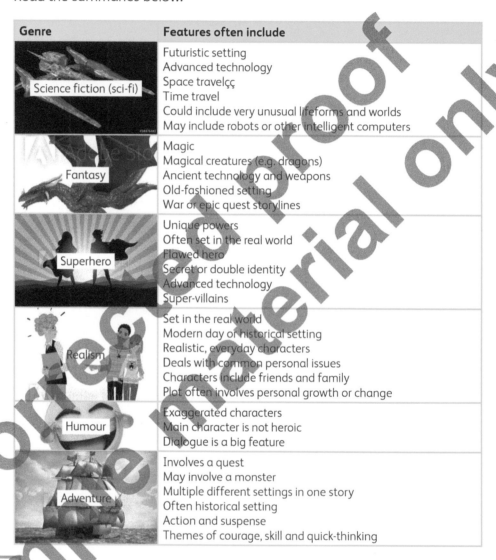

Genre	Features often include
Science fiction (sci-fi)	Futuristic setting Advanced technology Space travelçç Time travel Could include very unusual lifeforms and worlds May include robots or other intelligent computers
Fantasy	Magic Magical creatures (e.g. dragons) Ancient technology and weapons Old-fashioned setting War or epic quest storylines
Superhero	Unique powers Often set in the real world Flawed hero Secret or double identity Advanced technology Super-villains
Realism	Set in the real world Modern day or historical setting Realistic, everyday characters Deals with common personal issues Characters include friends and family Plot often involves personal growth or change
Humour	Exaggerated characters Main character is not heroic Dialogue is a big feature
Adventure	Involves a quest May involve a monster Multiple different settings in one story Often historical setting Action and suspense Themes of courage, skill and quick-thinking

EXTENSION

Work in a small group. Think of an example film and book for each genre in the table above. Can you think of a film or book that does not easily fit into one of these genres?

Activity 6.1

1 Think of three different books you have read. Which genres do they fit into?
2 Think of three different films or shows you have watched. Which genres do they fit into?
3 Do you have a preferred genre?

Readers making choices

Readers make choices about the books they pick from a shelf to read.

> My favourite stories are exciting and full of action.

> I like to read about characters like spies or detectives.

> I like to feel that other people share my issues and worries.

> It depends on my mood. Sometimes I like a world of magic and battles – other times I just like to be cheered up or laugh.

> I like to escape to different worlds.

Activity 6.2

1 Discuss the readers' comments above with a partner. Decide on the following:
   - Which genres do you think these readers are likely to pick?
   - Do you have any book or film suggestions for them?
   - Which person are you most like?
2 How do you choose a book to read or film to watch? What feelings and thoughts go into your decision?
3 Write a description of your favourite genres and explain your reasons. Use examples of the features from some specific films or books that you like.

Spotlight on: themes

Fiction in different genres can deal with different themes. These include:
- good vs evil
- loss
- friendship
- family
- growing up
- revenge
- power.

LET'S TALK

Think about the different stories or films you know well. What themes do they cover? A story may deal with more than one theme.

As a class, share your ideas about themes in fiction. Share your interpretations of themes in different films and books. Do you notice any patterns?

For example, do any themes appear more in certain genres?

What is the difference between theme and genre?

Writing and speaking

Personal viewpoints

Many people have strong opinions about genres.

 'Realism is more important because it deals with real issues. Other stories are just make-believe.'

 'Science fiction is the best because your imagination grows and grows.'

 'Superhero films are OK for young kids and teens, but I don't know why adults like them.'

Think about your own viewpoint about fiction.
- Do you strongly believe in one genre?
- Do you think a particular genre is over-rated?
- Do you think all genres are equal, but some stories are better than others?

Activity 6.3

Write a short speech giving your point of view and defending it with reasons.

Plan your speech by using a planning grid like this:

My viewpoint	Opening sentence	Examples of the fiction genres
Reason 1	Reason 2	Reason 3

Include suggestions for books or films that people could try for themselves.

Activity 6.4

Perform the speeches as a class.

When you are reading your speech, make sure that you read for the audience:
- make eye contact
- read clearly
- vary the tone and pitch of your voice to match the meaning of each sentence.

When you are listening:
- keep an open mind
- be sympathetic
- make eye contact.

Activity 6.5

Pair up with someone who has a different opinion from you and work together.
1 Read each other's speech in detail.
2 Discuss your opinions and summarise the main points.
3 Agree on some suggestions for books or films that the other person could try, in order to appreciate your viewpoint more fully.

EXTENSION

Work as a critical friend. Help your partner go through their speech.

Use the following prompts to give helpful feedback.

> A positive aspect of your speech is ...

> A positive aspect of how you performed your speech is ...

> One thing you should work on is ...

> Something I found interesting was ...

Key skills

Building detail in simple sentences

Writers use a range of sentence types in fiction writing.

They build the sentences to:
- show action
- describe settings
- express thoughts and feelings of characters
- build tension and suspense.

These simple sentences contain one main verb.

They can be especially effective in action sequences or to highlight a key description of a scene.

The ground shook.
The children ran.

The author has choices to build detail and be specific in simple sentences.

Verb choice

The ground shook.
The ground rumbled.
The ground groaned.
The ground cracked.
The ground trembled.
The ground split.

The children ran.
The children sprinted.
The children scampered.
The children scattered.
The children bundled away.
The children cowered.

Activity 6.6

1 Read each different version with a partner. Talk about the different effects from the verb change. Which would you choose if you were the author?

2 Think of different verb choices for these sentences. Write three different versions of each sentence by changing the verb.
- She **shouted** through the door.
- They **threw** stones and lumps of mud.
- The windows **smashed**.

> **HINT**
> A thesaurus is a useful tool for making word choices.

Add detail to the verb

Look at these different versions of simple sentences.

The ground shook violently.
The ground shook fiercely.
The ground shook with great force.
The ground shook beneath their feet.

The children scampered beneath the bushes.
The children scampered in every direction.
The children scampered in panic.
The children scampered, laughing and squealing happily.

HINT

Metaphors and similes can be built into simple sentences in fiction writing. For example:

The ground rumbled like a great sleeping bear.

The children scattered like sparks from a firework.

Her glance was as sharp as a piece of broken mirror.

The frozen lake was a mirror beneath their feet.

EXERCISE 6.1

Add detail to the main verb in these simple sentences:

1   The river flowed …
2   They listened …
3   The old house creaked …

EXERCISE 6.2

Search a fiction book. Look for simple sentences – sentences that have one clause, with one main verb.

Collect examples of simple sentences and copy them into your exercise book.

Now play with those sentences.

Write different versions of each sentence by:
■   changing the main verb
■   adding detail to the verb
■   using a simile to develop the verb.

She peered into the dark.

She peered fearfully into the dark.

She peered curiously into the dark.

On her hands and knees, she peered into the dark.

She peered into the dark, like a wise owl.

Share your favourite sentences with the class.

Challenge the class to guess the story, the genre and the author from just the collection of simple sentences you have found.

Reading

Compound and complex sentences in fiction

In Chapter 3, we looked at how compound sentences join two or more simple sentences with a conjunction (such as *and*, *but* or *so*).

Fiction writers often use commas in the place of a connective, to build a list of events or descriptions and get the story moving.

Look at these examples:

He glanced over his shoulder, gritted his teeth, clenched his fists and decided to run for it.

The town was quiet, everyone seemed friendly, neighbour waved to neighbour, but there was something not quite right.

The following extracts are from a short story, 'The Dragon Rock' by Ellena Ashley.

Author: Ellena Ashley

Ellena Ashley was born in England but emigrated to New Zealand in the 1970s when she was a teenager.

Extract: 'The Dragon Rock'

The ground began to rumble.

'Look out! Run! Run!'

The children scampered in all directions, shrieking and squealing, arms pumping with excitement.

The rumbling grew and grew.

The Dragon raised its sleepy head. It got onto its front feet and sat like a dog. It stood up and stretched, arching its long scaly back like a sleek tabby cat. It blinked and looked around with big kind, long lashed eyes.

And then its nostrils twitched and quivered again.

The older folk were alerted by the screams and shrieks. The ladies held up their long skirts to run and the men rolled their sleeves up and soon the whole town stood together in a tight huddle at the foot of the hill, staring up at the large beast with mouths held open.

'AHHHHH AAHHHHHHHHHH!!'

The noise erupted from the Dragon.

'AHHHHH AAHHHHHHHHHHHHHH!!'

The families gripped each other tighter and shut their eyes.

'AHHHHH CHOOOOOOOOO!!'

The sneeze blasted from the Dragon like a rocket, throwing it back fifty paces, causing a whirlwind of dust and dirt.

'AHHHHH CHOOOOOOOOOOOOOO!!'

The second blast split open the dry earth, sending explosions of soil and tree roots high into the sky like missiles, and something else too …

The people heard the sound but couldn't recognise it at first for it had been such a long time since their ears had heard such tinkling melody. As their eyes widened in wonder, their smiles turned into grins and then yahoos and hoorahs.

Water, cold, clear spring water, oozed, then trickled, then roared out of the hole, down the hillside and along the valley floor.

The torrent knocked over a farmer's haystack, but he didn't care.

The river carried away the schoolteacher's bike shed but she cared not a jot. It even demolished the Ladies' Bowling Club changing rooms but they howled with laughter and slapped their thighs. When the flood sent pools of water out towards the golf course, filling up sixteen of the eighteen holes, the men just hooted and whistled and threw their caps up in the air.

What used to be a dirty, brown dust bowl, now gleamed and glistened in the sunlight, sending playful waves and ripples across the lake and inviting all to share.

'HMMMMM,' sighed the Dragon sleepily, and showing his perfect movie star teeth. 'Seeing as I'm awake …'

And he lumbered forward with surprising grace and style and disappeared into the cool dark water with a small wave of a claw and flick of his tail.

Ellena Ashley

EXERCISE 6.3

Work with a partner.

1 How many times is the word *and* used in this extract?
2 Find and copy three examples of compound sentences.
3 Find and copy two different similes or metaphors.
4 Collect five interesting verb choices that you may use in your own writing.
5 Collect five other interesting vocabulary choices, copy them and write a definition of each word.

Compound-complex sentences

> When the flood sent pools of water out towards the golf course, filling up sixteen of the eighteen holes, the men just hooted and whistled and threw their caps up in the air.

This is an example of a **compound-complex** sentence.
- There is a dependent clause beginning 'When …'
- There are independent clauses linked with 'and'.

In fiction writing, you can vary your sentence types to build up detail.

Activity 6.7

Choose a page of a fiction book.

Find examples of these sentence types:
- simple
- compound
- complex
- compound-complex.

Copy them into a table like this:

Sentence type	Examples from fiction
Simple	They all nodded in agreement.
Compound	Farmers whistled lazily to themselves and would stand and stare into the distance.
Complex	Nobody was scared because it never, ever moved.
Compound-complex	After the families had restored and rebuilt the village, and set up sailing clubs for the children, and scuba diving for the grandparents, they erected a bandstand and monument in the spot where the dragon used to lay.
	Often on a cool night, when the stars were twinkling brightly in a velvet sky and the children were peacefully asleep, the grown-ups would settle for the evening with a mug of steaming cocoa in a soft cushioned armchair.

Activity 6.8

1 Think of more settings for each of the genres listed above. Complete a table like the one above.
2 Discuss possible settings for each of these genres:
  a realism
  b historical
  c humour.

Settings

The setting of a story is the place or places in which the events occur and the time when the story takes place. It is important that the setting is convincing and in keeping with the type of story being written. The mood or atmosphere are the emotional setting of the story.

Suitable settings for some different genres could be:

Sci-fi	Fantasy	Adventure
A spaceship Earth in the year 5000	A kingdom hidden in magical woodlands A dragon's cave	Inside an ancient ruin of a lost civilisation

Read these fiction extracts that give a setting.
Read out loud with a partner, taking it in turns.

Extract 1

As he approached, the city lights trembled in the distance and the low, constant rumble of traffic washed over him. He pulled his hood higher over his head as car lights swept past him, keeping to the shadows as much as he could. Passing the first houses there were no lights in the windows, tiles had slipped on the roof letting in the wind and the rain. A dog scampered across his path, its ribs clearly visible as it breathed.

Extract 2

The sun warmed my face as I skipped along the lane, clutching the present in my hands. I stopped to watch two young children shouting and squealing as their father shot water at them from a garden hose while they ran back and forth across the green grass, with droplets of the water shining like jewels in the evening light, creating mini rainbows in the spray. I checked my phone and, realising I was late, began skipping again.

Extract 3

In the pitch black I pressed my hand against the rock and took careful steps so I did not fall. The rock was damp on my hand, and I could hear water trickling somewhere beneath my feet. Ahead I could hear the water gain force and speed and begin to rumble like thunder.

Writing

Using setting to create an effect

A writer will not usually just tell you the setting. They do not say 'This story is on a spaceship and it is an adventure about going to a distant planet'. The writer gives clues by describing the objects, clothing and behaviour of people and animals.

EXERCISE 6.4

Answer each of these questions for each extract on page 100, using evidence from the text to support your thinking.

1   What clues does the writer give about the place?

2   What clues does the writer give about the time?

3   How does the writer set the mood?

4   What genre do you predict? Why?

5   Suggest what you think each story will be about.

EXERCISE 6.5

Now it's your turn to write your story setting.

You could choose from these different options, or think of your own:

- ■ an abandoned mine
- ■ an enchanted garden
- ■ a deserted factory
- ■ a family event.

Remember, to create a vivid setting you need to use clues in your descriptions to show the time and place, and to set the mood.

1   Write a version with a positive mood, using clues in the setting to show a positive, happy, safe or excited mood.

2   Now write a second version with the opposite mood. Change your descriptions so that the mood becomes tense, gloomy, scary or dangerous.

EXTENSION

Write a third version without any clues about the mood – keep the reader guessing!

KEY WORDS

third-person narrative (using 'he', 'she', etc.) the writer shows the thoughts and feelings of several characters

omniscient approach the narrator knows the thoughts and feelings of all of the characters in the story

first-person narrative (using 'I') telling the story from one character's point of view

Narration and point of view

A story can be told using a first-person (I) or a third-person narrator (who writes objectively using he, she, etc.).

A **third-person narrative** can focus closely on different characters and allows the author to build details and facts through more than one character. This is what is known as taking an **omniscient approach**.

On the other hand, a **first-person narrative** (using I) allows the author to build the mood by showing the thoughts and feelings of just one character, seeing the main events through their point of view.

A writer chooses whether to write in first person or third person.

Activity 6.9

Work with a partner.

1   Share your writing of a setting.
    Take it in turns to discuss these prompts:
    ■ Did you use first or third person?
    ■ Did you effectively describe a time and a place?
    ■ What could be done to improve the feeling or the mood?
    Discuss the strengths and weaknesses.

2   Take your partner's writing and rewrite it, adding improvements and changing the person.
    ■ If it was written in first person, change it to third person.
    ■ If it was written in third person, change it to first person.

3   Return the writing and show your new version to the partner. Discuss which changes you each like in the new versions, and which parts you would keep as originally written.
    ■ What was the effect of changing person?
    ■ Do you prefer the writing in the first person or the third person? Why?

Reading

Collecting extracts

Return to your debate about which types of book people in your class prefer.

Each person should have a book which is an example of one of their favourite kinds of fiction.

Activity 6.10

Find a short extract from the book – it should only be a few sentences long.
Look for passages of description rather than dialogue.

This extract should show:
- the setting as place
- setting in time
- the genre
- the mood.

1 Complete a table like this for your extract:

Title	
Author	
Genre	
Extract from page	
First sentence of extract	
Setting in time	
Setting in place	
Mood	
First person or third person	

2 Share your extract with a partner.
3 Discuss the techniques the author has used.
4 Share your personal response to your partner's text:
   A What do you notice about the language?
   B What do you wonder?
   C Does it draw you in and make you want to read the whole book? Why?

Reading as a writer

Now work as a class.

Your job is to introduce your extract to the class. They will need to know the following:
- the general background about the text and author
- the reason you chose the extract
- what writing skills it shows.

Activity 6.11

Give a short speech as an introduction to the extract you have chosen. Give some background information about the author, about the type of book, and then give some of your personal response to the writing.

It is important that your audience understands the style of writing, after they have listened to your speech.

While you listen to other people's speeches, take brief notes about each extract.

Zak's book – adventure – explorer history. Sounds exciting

Tamara's book – realism – mood is tense. Not heard of this author.

Activity 6.12

After the speeches, look through your notes. Which extracts sound interesting? Which sound like they are different from what you would normally read?

When you have been through your notes, ask for permission to read the extracts you thought sounded interesting. This will be an opportunity to read extracts from new authors, and to get some ideas for your own writing.

Add to your notes. Write down any sentences or phrases that draw you into the story, or that paint the setting very clearly.

Use these headings to help organise your ideas:
- Sentences that surprise or interest you
- Sentences that show mood
- Interesting new words
- Authors you have not heard of
- Books you may choose to read

Activity 6.13

Reflect on the extracts you have read.
- Which did you find appealed most to you?
- Were you surprised by anything?
- Have any of the extracts convinced you to try reading something new or different?

Write a brief reflection to describe your response to the different texts.

Share your findings in a class discussion.

Writing

Write your own story

Now it is time to put your fiction skills to work and write an episode yourself.

Writing fiction can be a daunting task. Some novels are over 1,000 pages long, and even writing a short story can take a professional writer months or years.

To develop your skills, you will write an episode from a story. It does not need to tell the whole story from beginning to end, but you will use it to build a setting and practise making decisions about the language you will use.

Activity 6.14

Have some fun thinking of a few different ideas for the genre and setting of your story. There is no pressure to choose the best or 'correct' idea. Just have fun making something up.

Step 1: Choose a setting

Step 2: Put a problem in your setting

For example:

On a beach, perhaps a huge hole has opened up in the sand, or there is a rockfall, or a huge wave.

A rope bridge may be the only way to reach safety, but some of the planks are broken.

The machines in the factory may be releasing steam and heat in a dangerous way.

At a party, perhaps the cake is too heavy to carry.

Step 3: Fill in some of the details

Make notes about the place, the people and the objects there.
Choose the mood you want to describe.

Step 4: Narrate

Choose first or third person for your first draft.

Now write!
Put a narrator or a character into the setting, and then put the problem in their way.
If they are at the family party, perhaps your narrator is the person who has to carry the heavy cake.
If they are on the beach, perhaps they are the ones who first realise the huge wave is coming.

You do not have to know how it will end. A first draft is a good way to find out what will happen.
You have a setting.
You have a problem.
You have a narrator.
Go!

Step 5: Review

A first draft is just the beginning. Read back through it or share it with a partner.

Use these prompts to think about the language choices you made:
- Where did you use simple, compound or complex sentences?
- How did you show the setting?
- How did your setting show the mood?
- Did you use first or third person? Would it be better if you switched?

Step 6: Rewrite

Use your language skills to make some more detailed choices about how to build detail into your sentences, how to build detail in the setting and generate an exciting and interesting episode.

Reviewing

Reflect on the short stories you have discussed, read and written in this chapter

Talk about:

- your thoughts on the debate about genre. Have you been introduced to any new genres you've never heard?
- how readers make different choices
- how writers can use narration as a tool
- what texts you have read that are similar to these.

If you like reading short stories, read these anthologies of short stories:

- *Winter Magic* by Abi Elphinstone
- *Dragons at Crumbling Castle: And Other Stories* by Terry Pratchett
- *Tales from Outer Suburbia* by Shaun Tan
- *Funny Girl: Funniest. Stories. Ever.* by Betsy Bird
- *Tales from India* by Bali Rai
- *Mystery and Mayhem* by Katherine Woodfine

What new authors would you choose?

Which authors would you recommend to others?

Reflect on your learning in this chapter

- What techniques have you learned to improve your reading, listening, speaking and writing?
- Make a list of things that you would like to practise further.
  - Compile a plan for tackling these.
  - Discuss your lists and ideas with a partner and your teacher.

All around the world

Reading

★ Excerpts from short stories and novels from the USA, Africa and Thailand
★ Poems from Jamaica and Japan

Speaking and listening

★ Listening to a conversation about food and culture
★ Talking about your own traditions and culture
★ Delivering a short presentation on culture

ALL AROUND THE WORLD

Writing

★ Writing a haiku
★ Using connectives in your writing
★ Varying sentence openers
★ Writing a formal article

Key skills

★ Non-standard English
★ Formal and informal language
★ Ellipses

LET'S TALK

Culture is all around us – it's in the language we speak, the clothes we wear, the food we eat, the music and songs we listen to, the games we play, and the movies we watch.

■ How does our culture influence the way we use language?

■ What texts or stories have you read that are from another culture?

■ Why do we read literature from different parts of the world?

■ How do you think authors use cultural context to better tell their stories?

Speaking and listening

Our culture, whether traditional or modern, influences how we behave in the world. It affects our values and attitudes, how we see ourselves and how we see, treat and relate to others. When we learn about other cultures, we deepen our understanding of others.

EXERCISE 7.1

1   Listen to a group of people talking about food in their culture. They live in different parts of Australia but they were not all born there. Their love of cooking has brought them together in a cooking competition.

2   As you listen, make notes about the names of the participants and where they come from. Then listen again and check your notes.

Activity 7.1

1   Working in a group, discuss what you understand by the word 'culture'.
2   What do you learn about each character's cultural background from the conversation you listened to?
3   What did you learn about these foods from the extract?
   ■ roti
   ■ dazhu gansi

▲ Roti   ▲ Dazhu gansi

4   What food would you prepare if you were asked to cook something you enjoy and which also represents your culture? Explain to your group what it is and say why it is important to you.

Reading and speaking

A short story set in the USA

Author: Amy Tan

Amy Tan was born in America but her parents were Chinese immigrants. She has written many novels including *The Joy Luck Club*.

EXERCISE 7.2

Before you read, skim the text and look at the illustrations and discuss these questions briefly with a partner.

1 Who are the main characters in this extract?

2 What game do they play?

3 Look at the first (opening) sentence in each paragraph for clues about content. For example, look at the first paragraph:

> On a cold spring afternoon, while walking home from school, I detoured through the playground at the end of our alley.

This gives you information about where and when the story is set and what the character is doing. It tells us the character is a school student.

4 Read the story with your partner. Take turns to read paragraphs.

▲ Life Savers are small colourful round sweets with a hole in the middle

Read the following extract, 'Rules of the Game'. The story is told by Meimei, who was born in the USA, where her parents emigrated from China.

Extract: 'Rules of the Game'

On a cold spring afternoon, while walking home from school, I detoured through the playground at the end of our alley. I saw a group of old men, two seated across a folding table playing a game of chess, others smoking pipes, eating peanuts and watching. I ran home and grabbed Vincent's chess set, which was bound in a cardboard box with rubber bands. I also carefully selected two prized rolls of sweets called Life Savers. I came back to the park and approached a man who was observing the game.

'Want to play?' I asked him. His face widened with surprise and he grinned as he looked at the box under my arm.

'Little sister, been a long time since I play with dolls,' he said, smiling **benevolently**. I quickly put the box down next to him on the bench and displayed my retort.

Spotlight on: cultural context

Texts have cultural context. Culture refers to a particular way of life, including the customs and traditions, beliefs, knowledge and behaviours of a particular group of people at a particular time.

WORD ATTACK SKILLS

Use your word attack skills to work out the meaning of the highlighted words by using the surrounding words:
✔ benevolently
✔ diminishing
✔ well-tended

Lau Po, as he allowed me to call him, turned out to be a much better player than my brothers. I lost many games and many Life Savers. But over the weeks, with each **diminishing** roll of candies, I added new secrets. Lau Po gave me the names. The Double Attack from the East and West Shores. Throwing Stones on the Drowning Man. The Sudden Meeting of the Clan. The Surprise from the Sleeping Guard. The Humble Servant Who Kills the King. Sand in the Eyes of Advancing Forces. A Double Killing Without Blood.

There were also the fine points of chess etiquette.

Keep captured men in neat rows, as **well-tended** prisoners. Never announce 'Check' with vanity, lest someone with an unseen sword slit your throat. Never hurl pieces into the sandbox after you have lost a game, because then you must find them again, by yourself, after apologising to all around you. By the end of summer, Lau Po had taught me all he knew, and I had become a better chess player.

A small weekend crowd of Chinese people and tourists would gather as I played and defeated my opponents one by one. My mother would join the crowds during these outdoor exhibition games. She sat proudly on the bench, telling my admirers with proper Chinese humility, 'Is luck.'

A man who watched me play in the park suggested that my mother allow me to play in local chess tournaments. My mother smiled graciously, an answer that meant nothing. I desperately wanted to go, but bit back my tongue. I knew she would not let me play among strangers. So as we walked home I said in a small voice that I didn't want to play in the local tournament. They would have American rules. If I lost, I would bring shame on my family.

'Is shame you fall down nobody push you,' said my mother. During my first tournament, my mother sat with me in the front row as I waited for my turn. I frequently bounced my legs to unstick them from the cold metal seat of the folding chair. When my name was called, I leapt up. My mother unwrapped something in her lap. It was her *chang*, a small tablet of red jade which held the sun's fire.

'Is luck,' she whispered and tucked it into my dress pocket. I turned to my opponent, a fifteen-year-old boy from Oakland. He looked at me, wrinkling his nose.

As I began to play, the boy disappeared, the colour ran out of the room and I saw only my white pieces and his black ones waiting on the other side. A light wind began blowing past my ears. It whispered secrets only I could hear.

'Blow from the South,' it murmured. 'The wind leaves no trail.' I saw a clear path, the traps to avoid. The crowd rustled. 'Shhh! Shhh!' said the corners of the room. The wind blew stronger. 'Throw sand from the East to distract him distract him.' The knight came forward ready for the sacrifice. The wind hissed, louder and louder. 'Blow, blow, blow. He cannot see. He is blind now. Make him lean away from the wind so he is easier to knock down.'

'Check,' I said, as the wind roared with laughter. The wind died down to little puffs, my own breath.

My mother placed my first trophy next to a new plastic chess set that the neighbourhood Tao society had given to me. As she wiped each piece with a soft cloth, she said, 'Next time win more, lose less.'

'Ma, it's not how many pieces you lose,' I said. 'Sometimes you need to lose pieces to get ahead.'

'Better to lose less, see if you really need.'

At the next tournament, I won again, but it was my mother who wore the triumphant grin.

'Lost eight piece this time. Last time was eleven. What I tell you? Better off lose less!' I was annoyed, but I couldn't say anything.

Amy Tan

LET'S TALK

This extract reflects on the attitudes of people of different generations. Meimei's parents grew up in China, whereas she has grown up in the USA.

1 Look at the way the writer tells the reader about her mother's (Ma's) cultural and social background.

She sat proudly on the bench, telling my admirers with proper Chinese humility, 'Is luck.'

This tells us that 'humility' and 'luck' are important in Chinese culture and important to Meimei's mother. What do you think Meimei thinks about this?

2 Find more examples from the extract which describe Ma and explain what they tell us about Ma's generation. Use these to explain the mother's attitude towards her daughter's interest in playing chess.

3 How does the writer show the tensions and differences between generations? Give examples to support your answers.

EXTENSION

1 Find out more about the rules of the game of chess. Explain the rules of the game to a classmate who does not know how to play it.

2 Explain how what Meimei's mother says after Meimei had won the game shows that her mother does not fully understand how the game is played.

EXERCISE 7.3

Answer these questions about 'Rules of the Game'.

1 What do you think the old man (Lau Po) means when he says, 'Little sister, been a long time since I play with dolls'?

2 What do you think Meimei's reason was for taking the Life Savers with her and why do you think that she lost so many of them?

3 Explain the meaning of 'fine points of chess etiquette' in your own words.

4 Why does Meimei think her mother will not allow her to play in the chess tournament?

5 Explain as fully as you can how Meimei managed to get her mother to approve of her playing in local chess tournaments.

6 What does the paragraph beginning 'As I began to play, the boy disappeared ...' tell you about Meimei's state of mind when she is playing chess?

7 How does Meimei's account of the game show that she had learned from Lau Po's teaching?

Key skills

Non-standard English

In the extract 'Rules of the Game', the author uses non-standard English to help the reader understand the cultural background of the mother and to build the voice of the writer.

Compare the non-standard English of the mother with standard English versions of the same sentences. What do you notice?

Non-standard English	Standard English
'Is luck,' she whispered.	'It is luck,' she whispered.
'Is shame you fall down nobody push you,' said my mother.	'It is a shame if you fall down when nobody pushes you,' said my mother.

KEY WORD

stanza a group of lines in a poem

Activity 7.2

1 Read the following poem aloud in pairs. Use the punctuation to guide you. Some ideas and sentences run over to the following line.
2 Talk about how the language changes in the poem in the second **stanza**. Is it formal or informal? Standard or non-standard?
3 Discuss how this language use reflects a modern culture and the voices of the poets.
4 Try writing the second stanza in formal English. Which version do you prefer? Why?

'Communication evolution'

Too slow and cumbersome
are the words of formal
English.
Slow dinosaurs, they lumber
around our
heads
engaging the mind
in a barrage of incomprehension,
leaving us shell-shocked,
blocking ideas,
hindering our communication.

Not so da words
of da
nu Generation.
Dey flow as kwik as
thoughts
creating bonds.
Evolved langwij,
Nu English.

Robert Asher and Chris Blackburn

Formal and informal language

We write friendly letters, blogs or posts to tell our family and friends about our lives. These written communications are usually quite informal because they are personal: we know the person with whom we are communicating (our audience).

Informal language may include:

- non-standard English (examples: *OK? Yip*)
- contractions (example: *don't* instead of *do not*)
- simple punctuation (examples: capital letters, full stops, commas, dashes, exclamation marks, ellipsis)
- incomplete sentences.

Reading and writing

Friendly letters

Activity 7.3

Look at the letter that Meimei has written to her cousin. Do you think it is formal or informal? Has she included all the features of a friendly letter?

Put your address at the top right corner. → 13 Garden Place
Fifth Street
New York, USA

Begin the letter with 'Dear' followed by the first name of the person to whom you are writing.

Add the date when you are writing. → 19 July 2021

Dear Meiling,

Organise your thoughts into paragraphs.

Sorry! Haven't written for such a long time. You'll never believe what's happened to me!

I started playing chess this summer — with the old men in the park. I used Vincent's old chess set. One amazing man, Lau Po, took me under his wing and taught me such a lot.

By the end of the summer, I took part in my first chess tournament — and I won! Yay! I didn't think that mother was going to let me play, but she even came to the tournament! Now I've won three trophies!

EXERCISE 7.4
Write an informal letter. Tell a friend about something that you did. Use informal language and the layout of a friendly letter.

I really love chess. I'll teach you when you come to visit in the fall, OK?

Your cousin,

Meimei

Reading

A story from Africa

<u>Author: Chinua Achebe</u>

Albert Chinualumogu Achebe (1930–2013) was an Igbo Nigerian novelist, poet and professor. His novel *Things Fall Apart* is the most read book in African literature.

EXERCISE 7.5

'Dead Men's Path' is a short story about a headmaster (Michael Obi, or Mike) who has progressive and modern ideas. He and his wife (Nancy) are attempting to change the school in Nigeria (Ndume School) where he has recently been appointed as headmaster.

Before you read, skim the text and discuss these questions with a partner.

1   Look at the first (opening) sentence in each paragraph for clues about content. Then discuss what you think this extract is about.

2   Read the story with your partner. What do you learn about the characters?

Spotlight on: register

The register of an extract can be formal or informal – or somewhere in between! An extract with a formal register will have more formal language: rich vocabulary, longer and varied sentences and precise punctuation.

KEY WORD

register how friendly (informal) or formal the language is that the characters use

'Dead Men's Path'

Michael Obi's hopes were fulfilled much earlier than he had expected. He was appointed headmaster of Ndume Central School in January 1949. It had always been an unprogressive school, so the Mission authorities decided to send a young and energetic man to run it. Obi accepted this responsibility with enthusiasm. He had many wonderful ideas and this was an opportunity to put them into practice. He had had sound secondary school education which designated him a 'pivotal teacher' in the official records and set him apart from the other headmasters in the mission field. He was outspoken in his condemnation of the narrow views of these older and often less-educated ones.

'We shall make a good job of it, shan't we?' he asked his young wife when they first heard the joyful news of his promotion.

'We shall do our best,' she replied. 'We shall have such beautiful gardens and everything will be just *modern* and delightful …'

In their two years of married life she had become completely infected by his passion for 'modern methods' and his denigration of 'these old and superannuated people in the teaching field who would be better employed as traders in the Onitsha market'. She began to see herself already as the admired wife of the young headmaster, the queen of the school.

The wives of the other teachers would envy her position. She would set the fashion in everything…Then, suddenly, it occurred to her that there might not be other wives. Wavering between hope and fear, she asked her husband, looking anxiously at him.

#211801149

'All our colleagues are young and unmarried,' he said with enthusiasm which for once she did not share. 'Which is a good thing,' he continued.

'Why?'

'Why? They will give all their time and energy to the school.'

Nancy was downcast. For a few minutes she became sceptical about the new school; but it was only for a few minutes. Her little personal misfortune could not blind her to her husband's happy prospects. She looked at him as he sat folded up in a chair. He was stoop-shouldered and looked frail. But he sometimes surprised people with sudden bursts of physical energy. In his present posture, however, all his bodily strength seemed to have retired behind his deep-set eyes, giving them an extraordinary power of penetration. He was only twenty-six, but looked thirty or more. On the whole, he was not unhandsome.

'A penny for your thoughts, Mike,' said Nancy after a while, imitating the woman's magazine she read.

'I was thinking what a grand opportunity we've got at last to show these people how a school should be run.' Ndume School was backward in every sense of the word. Mr Obi put his whole life into the work, and his wife hers too. He had two aims. A high standard of teaching was insisted upon, and the school compound was to be turned into a place of beauty. Nancy's dream-gardens came to life with the coming of the rains, and blossomed. Beautiful hibiscus and allamanda hedges in brilliant red and yellow marked out the carefully tended school compound from the rank neighbourhood bushes.

One evening as Obi was admiring his work he was scandalised to see an old woman from the village hobble right across the compound, through a marigold flower-bed and the hedges. On going up there he found faint signs of an almost disused path from the village across the school compound to the bush on the other side.

'It amazes me,' said Obi to one of his teachers who had been three years in the school, 'that you people allowed the villagers to make use of this footpath. It is simply incredible.'

'The path,' said the teacher apologetically, 'appears to be very important to them. Although it is hardly used, it connects the shrine with their place of burial.'

'And what has that got to do with the school?' asked the headmaster.

'Well, I don't know,' replied the other with a shrug of the shoulders. 'But I remember there was a big row some time ago when we attempted to close it.'

'That was some time ago. But it will not be used now,' said Obi as he walked away. 'What will the Government Education Officer think of this when he comes to inspect the school next week? The villagers might, for all I know, decide to use the schoolroom for a pagan ritual during the inspection.'

Heavy sticks were planted closely across the path at the two places where it entered and left the school premises. These were further strengthened with barbed wire.

Three days later the village priest or Ani called on the headmaster. He was an old man and walked with a slight stoop. He carried a stout walking-stick which he usually tapped on the floor, by way of emphasis, each time he made a new point in his argument.

'I have heard,' he said after the usual exchange of cordialities, 'that our ancestral footpath has recently been closed …'

'Yes,' replied Mr Obi. 'We cannot allow people to make a highway of our school compound.'

'Look here, my son,' said the priest bringing down his walking-stick, 'this path was here before you were born and before your father was born. The whole life of this village depends on it. Our dead relatives depart by it and our ancestors visit us by it. But most important, it is the path of children coming in to be born …'

Mr Obi listened with a satisfied smile on his face.

'The whole purpose of our school,' he said finally, 'is to eradicate just such beliefs as that. Dead men do not require footpaths. The whole idea is just fantastic. Our duty is to teach your children to laugh at such ideas.'

'What you say may be true,' replied the priest, 'but we follow the practices of our fathers. If you re-open the path we shall have nothing to quarrel about. What I always say is: let the hawk perch and let the eagle perch.' He rose to go.

'I am sorry,' said the young headmaster. 'But the school compound cannot be a thoroughfare. It is against our regulations. I would suggest your constructing another path, skirting our premises. We can even get our boys to help in building it. I don't suppose the ancestors will find the little detour too burdensome.'

'I have no more words to say,' said the old priest, already outside.

Two days later a young woman in the village died in childbed. A diviner was immediately consulted and he prescribed heavy sacrifices to propitiate ancestors insulted by the fence.

Obi woke up the next morning among the ruins of his work. The beautiful hedges were torn up not just near the path but right round the school, the flowers trampled to death and one of the school buildings pulled down … That day, the white Supervisor came to inspect the school and wrote a nasty report on the state of the premises but more seriously about the 'tribal war situation developing between the school and the village, arising in part from the misguided zeal of the new headmaster'.

Chinua Achebe

Activity 7.4

In this activity you will explore the language that Achebe uses.
1. An idiom is a figurative phrase that doesn't make sense in a literal way, but has a familiar meaning, such as 'over the moon' or 'cold feet'. What does the idiom 'A penny for your thoughts mean'?
2. Achebe's choice of words helps to paint a picture for the reader. Look at the paragraph beginning 'One evening as Obi …'. Find synonyms that Achebe has used for these words: shocked, walk, little. What is the effect of these words?
3. **Sibilance** can be used to create a calm feeling or to create a menacing feeling. What effect does it have in these lines from the extract?

Mr Obi listened with a satisfied smile on his face.

4. Comment on the use of connectives in the following sentences. What is the purpose? For example, to show a sequence, to compare or contrast ideas, or to add details? Do they make the language more formal or informal?

KEY WORD
sibilance the repetition of the 's' sound or 'sh' or 'ch' sounds

'Although it is hardly used, it connects the shrine with their place of burial.'
'… this path was here before you were born and before your father was born.'

OVERMATTER

Listening and reading

A story from Thailand

<u>Author: Khamsing Srinawk</u>

Khamsing Srinawk is a writer from the Isan region in Thailand. He was born in 1930 and is the best known short-story writer in Thailand.

Spotlight on: theme

The theme of a story is the main idea, lesson or message that stretches through the whole story: for example, suffering, survival, conflict, love, heroism, good and evil, or growing up.

WORD ATTACK SKILLS

Use your word attack skills to work out the meaning of the highlighted words.
- ✔ expanse
- ✔ pall

EXERCISE 7.6

Read this extract from 'The Gold-Legged Frog'. Nak, the main character, is thinking about recent events. Read the extract and think about what makes Nak's life so hard. Find examples to support your answer.

Extract: 'The Gold-Legged Frog'

The sun blazed as if determined to burn every living thing in the broad fields to a crisp. Now and again the tall, straight, isolated sabang and shorea trees let go of some of their dirty yellow leaves. He sat exhausted against a tree trunk, his dark blue shirt wet with sweat. The **expanse** round him expressed total dryness. He stared at the tufts of dull grass and bits of straw spinning in a column to the sky. The whirlwind sucked brown earth up into the air casting a dark **pall** over everything. He recalled the old people had told him this was the portent of drought, want, disaster, and death, and he was afraid. He was now anxious to get home; he could already see the tips of the bamboo thickets surrounding the house far ahead like blades of grass. But he hesitated. A moment before reaching the shade of the tree he felt his ears buzz and his eyes blur and knew it meant giddiness and sunstroke. He looked at the soles of his feet blistered from the burning sandy ground and became indescribably angry – angry at the weather capable of such endless torture. In the morning the cold had pierced his bones, but now it was so hot he felt his head would break into pieces. As he recalled the biting cold of the morning, he thought again of his little son.

Khamsing Srinawk

Activity 7.5

Listen to the story about what happened to the man's son. Discuss:
1 What was the attitude of the villagers? Were you surprised by this?
2 Was Nak concerned about his son? How was he persuaded to leave him?
3 Do you think Nak was lucky?

Reading and writing

A poem from Japan

A reader can learn about other cultures through poetry. The first poem you will read is translated from a Japanese haiku poem. It is about the tradition of stopping to gaze at the beauty of flowers, especially cherry blossoms and plum blossoms. This tradition is called *hanami*.

Poet: Kobayashi Issa

Kobayashi Issa, or just Issa as he is commonly known, lived from 1763 to 1828 in the Shinano Province of Japan.

He is known as one of the four greatest haiku poets.

Haiku

cherry blossoms scatter–
snap! the buck's antlers
come off

without regret
they fall and scatter…
cherry blossoms

cherry blossoms
fall! fall!
enough to fill my belly

cherry trees in bloom—
warmed by a brazier
blossom-gazing

Translation by David Gerard Lanoue

Why does the author use an ellipsis after 'scatter'? What is its effect?

WORD ATTACK SKILLS

Look up 'brazier' in a dictionary and write it in a new sentence. Find some synonyms you could use in your writing.

DID YOU KNOW?

Haiku is a traditional form of poetry from Japan. A haiku is usually about nature. It traditionally consists of 17 syllables written in one line or in three lines. There is no rhyming in the poem.

Activity 7.6

Discuss and answer these questions.
1. What does 'the buck's antlers' refer to in line 2?
2. How has the poet used punctuation to add to the effects in the poem?
3. What does the poem tell you about the cultural context of Japan?
4. What words are repeated? Why do you think they are repeated?
5. Why does the speaker say 'enough to fill my belly'? What do you think the speaker is doing at the time?
6. Does this poem follow the pattern of a traditional haiku?
7. Explain how the choice of form adds to the theme and cultural context.

Writing a haiku

EXERCISE 7.7

Water, plants and animals are very important in most cultures. Choose a photo from those below, or a cultural object from your family or community. Write a haiku to describe what it looks like and try to say something about why it is important in a culture.

You can write a traditional haiku with 17 syllables, like this:
- five syllables in the first line
- seven syllables in the second line
- five syllables in the third line.

Remember that you should use language precisely to express what you want to say.
- ■ Think of the imagery you want the reader to see and feel – so use literary and poetic devices to paint with words.
- ■ Follow the steps for planning, drafting, proofreading and finalising your haiku (see page v).

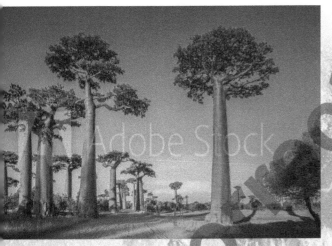

▲ Baobab trees are important in African culture

▲ Cows are treasured by many different cultures

▲ Waterfalls and the sea have a special place in many cultures

Poet: Kamau Brathwaite

Although the Honourable Edward Kamau Brathwaite was from Barbados, he lived in many countries around the world. He was a poet and academic, studying and writing about the cultural life of people of African descent in Africa and in the Americas.

Reading

A poem from the Caribbean

Activity 7.7

1 Work in pairs. Describe a pawpaw to your partner in three words.
2 Read the poem aloud. As you read, look ahead at the punctuation. This will help you to read the poem in a way that makes sense. Some sentences run on from one line to another.

The Pawpaw

Four little boys, tattered,
Fingers and faces splattered
With mud, had climbed
In the rain and caught
A pawpaw which they brought,
Like a bomb, to my house. I saw
Them coming: a serious, mumbling,
Tumbling bunch who stopped
At the steps in a hunch.
Releasing the fruit from the leaf
It was wrapped in, I watched them
Carefully wash the pawpaw
Like a nugget of gold. This done,
With rainwater, till it shone,
They climbed into the house
To present the present to me.
A mocking sign of the doom of all flesh
Or the purest gold in the kingdom?

Kamau Brathwaite

EXERCISE 7.8

1 In your own words, explain what you think the poem 'The Pawpaw' is about.
2 How would you describe the four little boys in 'The Pawpaw' to a friend?
3 Why do they wash the pawpaw like a nugget of gold?
4 Explain the two meanings of the word 'present' in 'The Pawpaw'.
5 What do you think the poet means in the last two lines of 'The Pawpaw'?
6 What does the 'The Pawpaw' show you about the cultural context of the 'me' and the four little boys in the poem?

Speaking

Making a presentation

So far, you have read stories and poems from other cultures around the world. You will now have an opportunity to deepen your understanding of your own culture while you prepare to make a short presentation about it.

Activity 7.8

Imagine that you have to choose three aspects of your culture to present to your future grandchildren, when they reach the age you are now. Which three things would you choose? Here are some examples, but do not be limited to these:

- typical customs and traditions of your culture
- food and festivals
- the clothes you wear
- songs, music, literature, dance or artworks
- beliefs and superstitions
- typical behaviours and values.

Prepare a talk on the three aspects you choose and present them to your class or group as if they were your own grandchildren. You can make notes for your presentation: keep these as you will use them in the writing activity that follows.

HINT

Think about your audience, especially how you can grab their attention and have an impact on them. You want them to remember what you are telling them.

- Don't make your presentation too long.
- Keep the register informal and make it fun.
- Change your voice to make it interesting. Add questions. Use short and long sentences.
- Provide interesting details.
- Use non-verbal ways to get attention too. Use pictures or demonstrate something by acting if you need to.

Writing

Building writing skills

In this unit you have read extracts from skilled authors and you have explored several ways in which they have created interesting texts that have an impact on the readers:

- using connectives
- varying the **sentence openers** in paragraphs
- using different registers.

Using connectives

We use connectives to build interesting and powerful paragraphs. A connective adds meaning to the paragraph as it can introduce additional information, make a sequence of events clear, make a comparison or give reasons and results. Connectives can be used as sentence openers or in the middle of sentences.

- Connectives such as *for, and, nor, but, or, yet* and *so* link independent (co-ordinating) clauses. These are not usually used at the beginning of a sentence.
- Connectives such as *because, although, until, if, when, while, before* and *after* are used to join an independent and dependent (subordinate) clause. They can be used at the beginning of a sentence.
- Connectives such as *first, then, after then* and *before* can be used as sentence openers and to connect clauses. They help us to sequence ideas.

EXERCISE 7.8

1 Look at the extracts you have read in this chapter. Find at least five examples of connectives. Copy the sentence in which each connective appears, and underline and label the connective.

2 Comment on why you think the author used this particular connective. What effect does it have in the story? What does it add to the purpose of the text?

3 Have a go at using connectives yourself. Connect then following sentences together. Remember that you can use a connective to start a sentence.

My sister and I usually walk to school together. She's a good walking partner. Sometimes she walks a bit fast for me. She always complains that I wake up late for school. I didn't wake up late this time! It was raining. I couldn't find my raincoat. I looked everywhere. I remembered I had left it at my friend's house the night before. There was no time to stop off to get it. I was going to get wet!

Varying sentence openers

Writers vary the way they start sentences to give variety to their writing and also to give emphasis to words in a sentence. Look at these examples from extracts you have read:

This phrase emphasises the time that it took Meimei to learn more about chess.

> By the end of summer, Lau Po had taught me all he knew, and I had become a better chess player.

Starting with this clause and the connective 'as' puts the emphasis on what Meimei is doing.

> As I began to play, the boy disappeared, the colour ran out of the room and I saw only my white pieces and his black ones waiting on the other side.

This gives emphasis to the way Obi feels and he wants others to know this too.

> 'It amazes me,' said Obi to one of his teachers who had been three years in the school, 'that you people allowed the villagers to make use of this footpath.'

Activity 7.9

Work in a pair. Try changing the way the following sentences begin to give a different emphasis. Share your ideas with another pair.

1 'Our ancestral footpath has recently been closed I have heard,' said the priest.
2 He was anxious to get home and see his son.
3 They carried the pawpaw like a bomb into my house.
4 The cherry blossoms fall to the ground without regret.

Formal register

You know that informal register may be created by using:

- non-standard English contractions
- punctuation (such as dashes, exclamation marks, ellipsis)
- incomplete sentences.

Formal register is created using formal language and complete sentences. Word choice can also be important. Look at these examples:

Informal	Formal
That's a great idea.	That is an excellent idea. /The idea is an excellent one.
Win more, lose less!	You should try to win more often and lose less often.
I'll teach you to play, OK?	If you would like to learn, I could teach you to play.

EXERCISE 7.10

Use the presentation that you made about aspects of your culture as a starting point. You wrote your notes in an informal register. Now use the same information to write a formal article. Focus on the paragraphs and the way you write them. Use connectives and vary the way you start sentences. Choose your words carefully.

Reviewing

Reflect on the texts you've read in this chapter

Talk about the texts you engaged with in this chapter.

- Which did you like?
- Which didn't you like?
- Which do you think were well-written? Why?
- What techniques did the authors or poets use to create effects in their writing?
- What stories, novels or poems have you read that are similar to these?
- what have you learnt about culture? have you learnt anything new about your own culture?

Ideas for further reading

If you want to read similar stories, here are some suggestions:

- *Some Places More Than Others* by Renée Watson
- *The Indian in the Cupboard* by Lynne Reid Banks
- *The Boy at the Back of the Class* by Onjali Rauf
- *No Ballet Shoes in Syria* by Catherine Bruton
- *I'm a Global Citizen: Culture and Diversity* by Georgia Amson-Bradshaw

Reflect on your learning in this chapter

Just as Meimei learned many different strategies to win at the game of chess, think of the strategies you have learned in this chapter to be a better reader – and a better writer!

- Make a list of things that you still need to master – or concepts with which you need more practice.
  - Compile a plan for tackling these.
  - Discuss your lists and ideas with your classmates and your teacher.

8 Poems aplenty

Reading
★ Finding themes in poems
★ Lyrical and narrative poems
★ Sonnets
★ How a poet uses voice
★ Persuasive poems

Speaking and listening
★ Listening for rhyme and rhythm
★ Listening for mood
★ Reading poems aloud
★ Listening for key events in poems

POEMS APLENTY

Writing
★ Creating atmosphere in a poem
★ Writing a poem about a fictitious person
★ Writing your own narrative or lyric poem
★ Writing a group poem with a theme

Key skills
★ Non-standard English
★ Formal and informal language
★ Ellipses

LET'S TALK

Throughout this book, we have looked at some poems as examples of different types of writing. Now, in this chapter, we will take a closer look at what poetry is and how it works.

■ What types of poems have you enjoyed so far? How have they made you feel?

■ How are poems different from other genres or text types?

■ How do you think poetry might have changed through the ages?

■ Do you know any poetic devices?

Speaking and listening

Poetry is one of the oldest forms of literature. Poets use structures and language together to create poems. The language of poetry is generally more concentrated than other forms of writing (such as short stories or novels) as poets pack as much meaning as possible into the language choices they make. You will explore how some poets do this in this chapter.

The structure and language of poetry

The structure of a poem is the way a poem is 'put together'. For example, a poem may consist of a few stanzas, each of the same length, for example four lines each. The poem may have a regular rhythm and rhyme too. The poem could also be written in **free verse**, which has no fixed structure.

Rhyme, rhythm and metre

In many poems, stressed **syllables** are organised into a regularly recurring **rhythm** (through repetition) to give the poem form and structure. A regular rhythmic pattern is known as the **metre** of a poem and is one of the main features that distinguishes poetry from **prose** – prose writing may have a rhythm but it doesn't usually have a metre. Much of the unique effect of poetry comes when poets combine a regular metre with a regular rhyming pattern.

Poetry also makes use of rhyme, which helps to create rhythm and makes poems easier to remember. This was important because the earliest forms of poetry such as ballads, were passed on by word of mouth from generation to generation.

EXERCISE 8.1

1. Look at the rhyme and rhythm in this extract of the poem 'The Walrus and the Carpenter' by Lewis Carroll. Describe the rhyming pattern and the rhythm of the poem.
2. Listen to the poem, focusing on the rhythm.
3. Read the poem aloud and try to capture the rhythm in the way you read.

Extract: 'The Walrus and the Carpenter'

But four young Oysters hurried <u>up</u>,	*a*
All eager for the <u>treat</u>:	*b*
Their coats were brushed, their faces <u>washed</u>,	*c*
Their shoes were clean and <u>neat</u> –	*b*
And this was odd, because, you <u>know</u>,	*d*
They hadn't any <u>feet</u>.	*b*

Lewis Carroll

KEY WORD

free verse a poem with no fixed or regular structure

Activity 8.1

Work in a group. If you have a favourite poem, quickly read or recite it to your group and say why you enjoy it.

KEY WORDS

syllable unit of sound (a beat) that can be a word on its own, e.g. *man*, but can be joined with other units of sound to form words, e.g. *woman*

metre the regular recurring rhythmic pattern of stressed and unstressed syllables on which a poem is based

prose a form of communication that uses ordinary grammar and flow

rhyme scheme the pattern of sounds that repeats at the end of a line or stanza (verse)

HINT

Each different rhyming word in a **rhyme scheme** is given an alphabet letter, for example, a, b, c, and so on.

Language and poetic devices

The language of a poem is the words that the poet chooses to use. Poets also use poetic devices such as onomatopoeia, alliteration, personification, sibilance, similes and metaphors to make the language even more meaningful. These poetic devices also emphasise the atmosphere, mood, and tone of a poem and they help to create the author's voice.

Poets repeat sounds in poems (though alliteration, **assonance** and sibilance, for example) to create an atmosphere, mood or rhythm. They use onomatopoeia to echo the meaning of words in their sound. This also adds to the mood and the rhythm of a poem.

> **KEY WORD**
>
> **assonance** the repetition of the same or similar vowel sounds within words, phrases or sentences

Extract: 'The Raven'

Once upon a midnight dreary, while I pondered, weak and weary,
Over many a quaint and curious volume of forgotten lore –
   While I nodded, nearly napping, suddenly there came a tapping,
As of some one gently rapping, rapping at my chamber door.
"Tis some visitor,' I muttered, 'tapping at my chamber door –
   Only this and nothing more.'

Edgar Allen Poe

Extract: *The Tempest*

ARIEL:
Hark, hark!
Bow-wow.
The watch-dogs bark!
Bow-wow.
Hark, hark! I hear
The strain of strutting chanticleer
Cry, 'cock-a-diddle-dow!'

William Shakespeare

EXERCISE 8.2

1 Listen to an extract of the poem 'The Raven'. Listen to the repeated sounds in the poem.

2 Give examples of alliteration and assonance in this extract from 'The Raven'.

3 Why has the poet used them? How do they add to the rhyme and rhythm of the poem?

Listen to an extract from one of Shakespeare's plays, *The Tempest*. In a group, discuss how onomatopoeia is used in this extract. Why does Shakespeare use it? How does it add to the meaning of the words?

Listening and reading

Conveying a theme and mood

KEY WORDS

mood the emotional setting; the feeling a reader gets when reading a poem

theme the content of a text: what a text is about

Activity 8.3

Listen to the poem 'Nature'. As you listen, think about the **mood** of the poem. Does it make you feel sad, happy, perhaps appreciative? Discuss in a pair and refer to the words in the poem to explain your answer.

Poet: HD Carberry

Although Hugh Doston Carberry (1921–89) was born in Canada, he was taken to Jamaica where he spent most of his life.

'Nature'

We have neither summer nor winter
Neither autumn nor spring.
We have instead the days
When gold sun shines on the lush green canefields –
Magnificently.
The days when the rain beats like bullets on the roofs
And there is no sound but the swish of water in the gullies
And trees struggling in the high Jamaica winds.

Also there are the days
when the leaves fade from off guango trees
And the reaped canefields lie bare and fallow in the sun.
But best of all there are the days when the mango and the logwood blossom.
When the bushes are full of the sound of bees and the scent of honey,
When the tall grass sways and shivers to the slightest breath of air,
When the buttercups have paved the earth with yellow stars
And beauty comes suddenly and the rains have gone.

HD Carberry

EXERCISE 8.3

Think about the theme of this poem and how the writer makes an impact on the reader through choice of words and the use of poetic devices.

1   Explain what the following words and phrases mean as they are used in the poem, 'Nature': *lush, swish, gullies, fallow*.

2   What images does the poet use in 'Nature' to describe the sun, the canefields and the rain. Refer to the words he uses.

3   Carberry uses a simile and metaphors in 'Nature' to make comparisons. Find these and explain the comparisons. Are the comparisons effective? How do they add to your understanding of the poem?

4   Give two examples of personification. How do they add to the meaning of the poem?

HINT

Remember that a simile is a direct comparison introduced by 'like' or 'as'. A metaphor is an indirect comparison in which it is implied that one thing is like another.

Reading and listening

Types (forms) of poems

Although all poems are unique and all poets are individual, there are different types (or forms) of poetry: lyrical (non-narrative) and narrative.

Lyrical poems are usually quite short and concentrated. Most lyrical poems are concerned with conveying strong feelings inspired by a particular experience – it could be love, or sadness or even the effect of listening to a bird singing.

A **narrative poem** is, as the name suggests, a poem that tells a story. A ballad is a type of narrative poem. Narrative poems are often quite long with less concentrated language than lyrical poems. Narrative poetry can also be used in plays, like for example in the plays of Shakespeare. This is also called dramatic poetry.

> **DID YOU KNOW?**
> The word 'lyrical' comes from the old musical instrument called a 'lyre' and originally meant a poem that could be set to music.

> **KEY WORDS**
> **lyrical (non-narrative) poem** a poem about a particular experience, usually showing strong feelings in a short form
> **narrative poem** a poem that tells a story

Activity 8.4

Listen to the extract from 'My heart leaps up when I behold' and discuss these questions in a pair.

1 Is this a lyrical poem or a narrative poem? Discuss why you think this.
2 What sort of language has the poet used? Why do you think the poet chose to use this language?
3 What can you say about the word order the poet has used? Is this the way you would express things?
4 Discuss what this poem is about.

Poet: William Wordsworth

William Wordsworth (1770-1850) was an English romantic poet. He wrote many lyrical poems and ballads.

'My heart leaps up when I behold'

My heart leaps up when I behold
    A rainbow in the sky:
So was it when my life began;
So it is now I am a man;
So be it when I shall grow old,
    Or let me die!
The Child is father of the Man;
And I could wish my days to be
Bound each to each by natural piety.

William Wordsworth

KEY WORD

sonnet a form of poem that always has 14 lines

A Shakespearian sonnet

Sonnets are special kinds of lyrical poems that have only 14 lines. Usually the first 8 lines contain a main idea that changes in the following 6 lines.

Activity 8.5

1   Listen to the following sonnet, which is by William Shakespeare, and say briefly what you think it is about.
2   Read the sonnet. In what way does Shakespeare compare the person and the summer's day in the poem?

'Shall I compare thee to a summer's day?'

Shall I compare thee to a summer's day?
Thou art more lovely and more temperate:
Rough winds do shake the darling buds of May,
And summer's lease hath all too short a date:
Sometime too hot the eye of heaven shines,
And often is his gold complexion dimm'd;
And every fair from fair sometime declines,
By chance or nature's changing course untrimm'd;
But thy eternal summer shall not fade,
Nor lose possession of that fair thou ow'st;
Nor shall death brag thou wander'st in his shade,
When in eternal lines to time thou grow'st:
So long as men can breathe or eyes can see,
So long lives this, and this gives life to thee.

William Shakespeare

Activity 8.6

1   Find an example of a modern sonnet and read it aloud to your group or class.
2   How did you choose this sonnet? Did you look at the theme or the structure?
3   What do you prefer, the modern sonnet or the Shakespearian sonnet? Can you say why?

EXERCISE 8.4

Now look at the structure of the sonnet. Shakespeare and other English writers at the time (the late 16th and early 17th centuries) developed their own unique forms for sonnets.

1   Look at the first four lines of the sonnet. Do they rhyme? How many syllables are there in each line?
2   Can you find other sections of the poem that have a similar structure?
3   Look at the last two lines of the poem. Comment on the layout, the number of syllables and the rhyme.

EXTENSION

1   Find some examples of modern sonnets and discuss their structure, rhyme and rhythm.
2   Find examples of other types of lyrical poems and share a few with the class.

Reading and speaking

A lyrical poem in free verse

Activity 8.7

1 Read the poem aloud in a pair or small group.
2 Listen to the poem. Did your reading sound similar to the recording? Try reading the poem again.
3 Look at the way the poet structures her sentences. Why do you think she uses 'and' so many times?

HINT

Use the punctuation to guide you. The poet has used enjambment (lines of poetry that run on from one line to the next) in this poem, so you need to read ahead as you read aloud to make sense of the content.

Poet:
Jenny Joseph

Jenny Joseph (1932–2018) was an English poet.

LET'S TALK

1 What is the main idea of the poem 'Warning'?
2 Why do you think the author wrote it?
3 Who do you think this poem appeals to?
4 Did you enjoy the poem? What was its impact on you, the reader?

'Warning'

When I am an old woman I shall wear purple
With a red hat which doesn't go, and doesn't suit me.
And I shall spend my pension on brandy and summer gloves
And satin sandals, and say we've no money for butter.
I shall sit down on the pavement when I'm tired
And gobble up samples in shops and press alarm bells
And run my stick along the public railings
And make up for the sobriety of my youth.
I shall go out in my slippers in the rain
And pick flowers in other people's gardens
And learn to spit.

You can wear terrible shirts and grow more fat
And eat three pounds of sausages at a go
Or only bread and pickle for a week
And hoard pens and pencils and beermats and things in boxes.

But now we must have clothes that keep us dry
And pay our rent and not swear in the street
And set a good example for the children.
We must have friends to dinner and read the papers.

But maybe I ought to practise a little now?
So people who know me are not too shocked and surprised
When suddenly I am old, and start to wear purple.

Jenny Joseph

Why do you think the poet chose to use a free verse structure? Does it enhance the meaning of the poem?

EXERCISE 8.5

1 Why do you think Jenny Joseph called her poem 'Warning'?
2 Explain in your own words some of the things that she plans to do when she grows old and why these are likely to shock people.
3 What is meant by the line 'And make up for the sobriety of my youth'?
4 Who is the 'you' and 'us' the poet is referring to?
5 Why does the narrator of the poem think that she ought to practise now?

Speaking and writing

A lyrical poem with atmosphere

Activity 8.8

1   Listen to the poem 'Stopping by Woods on a Snowy Evening'. As you listen, think about how the poet uses language to convey **atmosphere**.
   - Think about the choice of words.
   - What are poetic devices? Can you hear any?
2   Discuss and comment on the structure of this poem.
   - How many stanzas are there? Are they all the same length?
   - Is there a rhyme scheme? What effect does this have?
3   Now look at the punctuation.
   - Why does the poet use a semi-colon after 'though'?
   - What is the effect of **enjambment** in this poem?

Poet: Robert Frost

Robert Frost (1874-1963) was an American poet. He received four Pulitzer Prizes for Poetry.

'Stopping by Woods on a Snowy Evening'

Whose woods these are I think I know.
His house is in the village though;
He will not see me stopping here
To watch his woods fill up with snow.

My little horse must think it queer
To stop without a farmhouse near
Between the woods and frozen lake
The darkest evening of the year.

He gives his harness bells a shake
To ask if there is some mistake.
The only other sound's the sweep
Of easy wind and downy flake.

The woods are lovely, dark and deep,
But I have promises to keep,
And miles to go before I sleep,
And miles to go before I sleep.

Robert Frost

KEY WORD

atmosphere how the physical situation or environment feels
enjambment a term used to describe lines of poetry that run on from one line to the next without a pause

LET'S TALK

Discuss whether or not 'Stopping by Woods on a Snowy Evening' has another figurative meaning. When you are discussing, remember to:

- make sure that everyone has a turn to speak
- identify points of agreement and disagreement in opposing points of view
- take notes and report back to the class on your conclusions.

LONG PAGE

EXERCISE 8.6

1   Write one stanza of a poem to describe the atmosphere of a place that you like to go to. To give the poem some impact, use:
   - a regular structure with rhyme
   - at least one poetic device (alliteration, simile, etc.)
   - punctuation such as commas, colons, semi-colons and full stops.

Poet: Edna St Vincent Millay

Edna St Vincent Millay (1892–1949) was a poet and playwright. She was born in Maine in the USA and received the Pulitzer Prize for Poetry in 1923. She wrote many lyrical poems.

Spotlight on: tone

The tone of a poem is the writer's attitude toward the theme of the poem. A writer may be playful, for example, or regretful. The tone of a poem can change during a poem.

LET'S TALK

Some people think that the little ghost is really the child part of the poet that she has lost. What do you think?

Reading

Narrative poems

You will remember from Chapter 5 that poems can be narratives: in other words, they can tell stories. In Chapter 5 you read ballads. Now you will read and listen to some different narrative poems.

Activity 8.9

1 Before you read this poem, look at the structure quickly and describe it. How many stanzas are there? Do they each have the same number of lines? Is there rhyme?

2 What do you think the poem is about?

'The Little Ghost'

I knew her for a little ghost
That in my garden walked;
The wall is high – higher than most –
And the green gate was locked.

And yet I did not think of that
Till after she was gone –
I knew her by the broad white hat,
All ruffled, she had on.

By the dear ruffles round her feet,
By her small hands that hung
In their lace mitts, austere and sweet,
Her gown's white folds among.

I watched to see if she would stay,
What she would do – and oh!
She looked as if she liked the way

I let my garden grow!
She bent above my favourite mint
With conscious garden grace,
She smiled and smiled – there was no hint
Of sadness in her face.

She held her gown on either side
To let her slippers show,
And up the walk she went with pride,
The way great ladies go.

And where the wall is built in new
And is of ivy bare
She paused – then opened and passed through
A gate that once was there.

Edna St Vincent Millay

EXERCISE 8.7

1 Explain what this poem is about in two sentences. Say who it is about and what you learn about this character.

2 What effect does the alliteration in this poem have?

3 Look at how the writer uses dashes. What effect do these dashes have on the way you would read the poem?

4 What is this tone of this poem? Think about how you would read it aloud.

Spotlight on: an author's voice

An author's voice is developed through the style in which an author writes – the structure of sentences, the choice of words and the tone of the writing of writing. You may remember the voice of Gerald Durrell in the extracts you read of his writing.

Listening and reading

An author's voice

Activity 8.10

1 Listen to the poem 'The Listeners'. Don't worry if you do not understand every word you hear. Try to get a feel for the mood, atmosphere and tone of the poem.
2 This is a narrative poem. Can you explain the events described?

Poet: Walter de la Mare

Walter de la Mare (1873-1956) was an English poet, born in Kent in the south-east of England. He also wrote short stories and novels.

WORD ATTACK SKILLS

Work out the meaning of the highlighted words in the context of the poem.
✔ champed
✔ turret
✔ smote
✔ perplexed
✔ thronging
✔ hearkening
✔ spake
Then check their meaning in a dictionary. How many of these words do you think are old and rarely used today?

'The Listeners'

'Is there anybody there?' said the Traveller,
Knocking on the moonlit door;
And his horse in the silence champed the grass
Of the forest's ferny floor;
And a bird flew up out of the turret,
Above the Traveller's head:
And he smote upon the door again a second time;
'Is there anybody there?' he said.
But no one descended to the Traveller;
No head from the leaf-fringed sill
Leaned over and looked into his grey eyes,
Where he stood perplexed and still.
But only a host of phantom listeners
That dwelt in the lone house then
Stood listening in the quiet of the moonlight
To that voice from the world of men:
Stood thronging the faint moonbeams on the dark stair,
That goes down to the empty hall,
Hearkening in an air stirred and shaken
By the lonely Traveller's call.
And he felt in his heart their strangeness,

➡

Some people think
that the house in 'The
Listeners' represents
the loneliness and
emptiness that some
people feel. What do
you think?

KEY WORDS

colon (:) introduces
something that is to
follow

semi-colon (;) links
two independent
clauses and can
be used between
sentences that have
a common theme to
create a pause and
emphasis effect, like
the effect of a full
stop

comma (,) separates
information or some
clauses and items in
a list

LET'S TALK

Compare the two
poems: 'Silver' and
'The Listeners' by
Walter de la Mare.

■ What can you say
about the poet's
distinctive voice?

■ Are the poems
similar in their use
of imagery, mood,
rhythm or rhyme?

■ What language
does the poet
use? What impact
does it have on
the reader?

**WORD ATTACK
SKILLS**

What is the meaning
of these words in the
poem?

✔ shoon
✔ casements
✔ cote

Their stillness answering his cry,

While his horse moved, cropping the dark turf,

'Neath the starred and leafy sky;

For he suddenly smote on the door, even

Louder, and lifted his head:–

'Tell them I came, and no one answered,

That I kept my word,' he said.

Never the least stir made the listeners,

Though every word he spake

Fell echoing through the shadowiness of the still house

From the one man left awake:

Ay, they heard his foot upon the stirrup,

And the sound of iron on stone,

And how the silence surged softly backward,

When the plunging hoofs were gone.

Walter de la Mare

Activity 8.11

Discuss how Walter de la Mare uses punctuation to create effects in 'The
Listeners'.

1   Find examples of colons and semi-colons in the poem, and discuss why
the poet has used them (for example, the semi-colon after 'sky' and the
dash and colon after 'head').

2   How would you read the sentences below? Why has the poet not
added punctuation after the word 'grass'? What do you call this? Can
you find other examples in the poem?

*And his horse in the silence champed the grass
Of the forest's ferny floor;*

EXERCISE 8.8

You are going to listen to the poem 'Silver' by Walter de la Mare.

1   First, look at the picture and guess what the poem might be about. Once
you have heard the poem, discuss what you think the poem is about. What
kind of poem is it – narrative or lyrical?

2   Listen again and talk about the rhythm of the poem. Did you hear any
rhyming, alliteration or assonance?

3   Read the following lines from the poem. What poetic devices has the poet
used here? What effect does this have?

Slowly, silently, now the moon
Walks the night in her silver shoon;
This way, and that, she peers, and sees ...

4   What is the rhyme scheme of the poem?

5   Give one example of alliteration and one of
assonance from the poem.

6   Why does the poet use a semi-colon after 'shoon'?

LONG PAGE

Reading and writing

Describing characters in poetry

Poet: Brian Patten

Brian Patten (born in 1946) is an English poet and author. He often writes lyrical poetry about human relationships.

EXERCISE 8.9

The next two poems are both about schoolteachers and how they affect the children in their classes. Read both poems carefully.

'Geography Lesson'

Our teacher told us one day he would leave
And sail across a warm blue sea,
To places he had only known from maps,
And all his life had longed to be.

The house he lived in was narrow and gray
But in his mind's eye he could see
Sweet-scented jasmine clambering up the walls,
And green leaves burning on an orange tree.

He spoke of the lands he longed to visit,
Where it was never drab or cold.
And I couldn't understand why he never left,
And shook off our school's stranglehold.

Then half-way through his final term
He took ill and he never returned,
And he never got to that place on the map
Where the green leaves of the orange trees burned.

The maps were pulled down from the classroom wall;
His name was forgotten, it faded away.
But a lesson he never knew he taught
Is with me to this day.

I travel to where the green leaves burn,
To where the ocean's glass-clear and blue,
To all those places my teacher taught me to love –
But which he never knew.

Brian Patten

Poet: Robert Pottle

Robert Pottle is a children's poet. He grew up in Eastport, Maine in the USA. He worked as a first-grade (the same as Year 2) teacher.

'Black Beard'

He angrily barks out his orders.
His face wears a permanent scowl.
And if you should ask him a question
His only response is to growl.

His discipline methods are ruthless.
He believes in all work and no play.
And if you should happen to step out of line
It may be with your life you will pay.

I'd rather an octopus hug me.
I'd rather have sharks bite my rear
Than to walk into class on the first day of school
To find Black Beard's my teacher this year.

Robert Pottle

LET'S TALK

Poets use words and language to express emotions and to create mood or atmosphere. In what tone of voice would the poet read the poem? What voices might you use for the different characters in the poems on these two pages? Some examples of tone of voice are serious, flippant, quiet, loud, dramatic and bold.

EXERCISE 8.10

Write a comparison of the two poems 'Geography Lesson' and 'Black Beard', in which you look at ways in which they are similar and ways in which they are different. You should think about:
- what the teachers are like and what you learn of their lives
- the effect the teachers have on their students
- the words the poets use to create their pictures of the teachers
- the structures of the poems (punctuation, stanzas and rhyming) and how they help to emphasise key words
- how the poets use phonetic devices such as alliteration and assonance
- how the poets use similes, metaphors and personification.

EXERCISE 8.11

Write your own poem about a fictitious teacher that everyone loves. Copy and complete the table below as an aid to plan your poem.
- Think about the form and structure you want to use. Do you want a regular pattern of rhyme or not?
- Use descriptive words to create a picture of the teacher and phonetic repetition such as alliteration, assonance and sibilance.

	Descriptive words I can use
What the teacher is like	
Effect on learners	
What you know about the teacher's life and dreams	
Your opinion of the teacher	

LONG PAGE

Activity 8.12

1 Read your poem to a partner or to your group. Explain what tone you tried to create and which words you used to help.
2 Take turns to give each other feedback about the poems. Comment on the structure and language, and say how the poem made you feel.

139

Poet: Medora Chevalier

Medora Chevalier is a well-known writer, poet and commentator on what is happening in our world today. She is a choreographer and dancer and has performed poetry for many festivals for human rights, peace and Earth Day.

Spotlight on: purpose

What is the purpose of the poem? Why did the poet write it? What did she hope to achieve? Do you think it is successful?

EXERCISE 8.12

Answer these questions about the poem 'Or Will the Dreamer Wake?'.

1   What does Chevalier mean by 'These cubs could be the last ones ever/To freely live and roam and mate'?

2   What will the 'grandchild' in each stanza never know?

3   Why does the poet ask, 'will the dreamer wake?' Why is this question repeated? Does the poet expect an answer to this kind of question?

4   What is the poet's tone in this poem?

5   How does the poet use emotive language to persuade people? Give two examples.

WORD ATTACK SKILLS

What do you think these words mean as they are used in the poem?
- ✓ plaintive
- ✓ warbles
- ✓ snuffles
- ✓ clutch
- ✓ gleaming

Speaking and reading

Using poetry to persuade

Activity 8.13

1   Listen to the poem 'Or Will the Dreamer Wake?' carefully.
2   What is this poem about? Who is the 'the dreamer'?
3   What question does the poet repeat?
4   What is the purpose of this poem?

Extract: 'Or Will the Dreamer Wake?'

Out in the East the jungle listens
The tigress, plaintive, growls in pain,
The great trees hear her breathing, shaking
Inside her still, the new lives wait.
These cubs could be the last ones ever
To freely live and roam and mate.
Our grandchild knows the tiger never
Or will the dreamer wake?
Far in the North the white bear snuffles
Down in her lair the gleaming snow
She waits for all the life she's making
Outside the crashing glaciers grow.
These cubs could be the last cubs ever
To freely live and roam and mate.
Our grandchild knows the white bear never
Or will the dreamer wake?
There in the West the song thrush warbles
She weaves her nest to hold her clutch
A long wait now to find a partner
The eggs are laid, there are not much.
These chicks could be the last ones ever
The last to fly and sing and mate.
Our grandchild knows the song thrush never
Or will the dreamer wake?

photo 08_27 is corrupt.
Please resupply

Medora Chevalier

EXERCISE 8.13

Now read the following poem, which was inspired both by the poet's love of whales and by their senseless slaughter.

Poet: Cheryl Kaye Tardif

Cheryl Kaye Tardif (born in 1963) is an international bestselling author. She has written poetry, scripts and novels.

Extract: 'A Whale Song'

Amidst the ocean depths, far below the light,
A lone whale glides by in her watery flight.
A cry so lonely, a wailing of despair,
Something precious lost in the great somewhere.
Serene, yet watchful, moving always in fear
Of death's stillness, she searches ever near.
Pulling sunlight upward with care,
She caresses the surface and mists the salty air.

Nothing! Not a movement, except a hulking mass,
A predator's scent, a watchful, sweeping pass.
Dangerously taunting, the sight draws her near
As battered nets pull in Death and despair.

Her baby! Her angel! Death had claimed its song,
While a quiet stillness seemed to linger on.
Across the endless ocean, far below the sky,
A mournful mother sang a haunting lullaby.

Cheryl Kaye Tardif

> Explain what this figure of speech means.

> What is the effect of the alliteration in this line?

WORD ATTACK SKILLS

What do these words mean as they are used in the poem?
- ✔ wailing
- ✔ serene
- ✔ predator
- ✔ taunting

EXERCISE 8.14

Answer these questions about 'A Whale Song'.

1 What does the 'hulking mass' refer to?
2 What does the poet mean by, 'Her baby! Her angel! Death had claimed its song.'?
3 Identify two senses the poet draws on to create a picture in our minds. Refer to the words or phrases she uses.
4 Explain the last line, 'A mournful mother sang a haunting lullaby.'
5 What is the pattern of rhyme in the poem? What effect does this have, combined with the alliteration?
6 What is the impact of the poem? How does this link to the poem's purpose?

Listening and speaking

HINT

Enjoyment is the key here. Choose poems that you like.

Use your voice – stress different words, vary the speed of reading, pause, read softy and loudly in parts.

Use gestures and movements to add meaning to what you are reading aloud.

Act out the poem as you read if you think it adds to the enjoyment and understanding for your audience.

Activity 8.14

1 Working in a small group of three or four, find two more poems that as a group you enjoy reading – you could choose other poems by some of the poets you have encountered in this chapter.
2 As a group, introduce your poems to the class and read them aloud (perhaps reading verses in turn). Remember to use the punctuation as a guide for when to have small and long pauses.
3 Explain what it is you like about the poems.

Activity 8.15

Play this game and create a poem in a group. All you need is some inspiration, a sheet of paper and a pen or pencil for each person in your group.

1 Choose a theme, for example, 'nature', 'having fun', 'silence'. Think about the poems you have read in this unit.
2 Each person in the group finds a picture related to the theme. Take a few minutes to look at your own picture, but don't talk yet.
3 Sit in a circle. Place your pen, paper and your picture in front of you. Move one place to the left.
4 Look at the picture in front of you now. Write a sentence or a few words about it on the paper in front of the picture.
5 Fold the paper over so that the next person can't see what you have written and leave the paper there.
6 Move another place to the left and do the same for the next picture. Write a sentence about it on the piece of paper in front of the picture. Repeat until you have written words or lines on each sheet, ending with your own sheet.
7 Each person opens the sheet of paper and reads aloud the poem on their sheet, which make up a poem.
9 Discuss the poems you have created as a group.

Unexpected patterns
White icicles and frost
Shivering silent scenes
Time to explore
Put on your caps and scarves

photo 08_31 is corrupt. Please resupply

Writing

EXERCISE 8.15

Write your own narrative or lyrical poem.

HOW TO START
- Choose a theme to write about.
  - You can use the poems that were created for you in the game you played as a starting point, or you can choose something different.
- Free-write about your theme.
- Read or listen to other poems on this theme.

PLAN YOUR POEM
- Decide on the form and structure of your poem. Will you use rhyme and stanzas or will you write in free verse?
- What tone do you want to set?
- Will your poem have a purpose, for example, to persuade?

DRAFT AND ENHANCE
- Write a few lines or just a few words.
- Add poetic devices to add detail and meaning. Try adding a simile. Then add alliteration or assonance.
- Add punctuation or use enjambment.
- You could read your poem aloud to a partner and ask for feedback.

Use this checklist to make sure you have covered all the details needed in your poem.

	Check
Planning	
▪ Used various sources for inspiration?	
Structure	
▪ Stanzas and lines or free verse used for a purpose?	
▪ Punctuated effectively?	
Language	
▪ Spelled properly?	
▪ Well-chosen and interesting?	
▪ Poetic devices used to create meaning and rhythm?	
My voice and style	
▪ Right for this kind of poem?	

EXTENSION

Rhyme, rhythm and repetition are not only used in poetry, they are also used in rap. Good rap has a structure; the words are well organised, they work closely and well together; there is a rhythm that others can follow and there is repetition of words.

Rap as we know it today originated in New York. Do some quick research online about the history of rap. Share examples of raps you like between yourselves, if you have any. If you're not sure where to start, your teacher can advise.

As a group, write and perform a rap. Then have a rap battle between the groups.

Reviewing

Reflect on the poems you've read in this chapter

Talk about:
- which poems you liked and which you didn't like
- which you think were well-written and why
- what techniques the poets used to create effects in their writing
- how you found writing your own poem. What did you find difficult or easy?
- how you found writing a group poem around a theme. Did you prefer to collaborate on poetry or write alone?

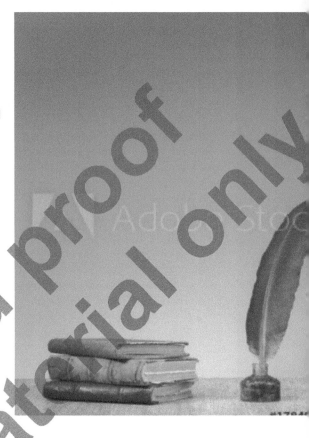

If you like nonsense narrative verse, read:
- 'Jabberwocky' by Lewis Carroll
- 'The Marrog' by RC Scriven

If you like reading poetry, try these anthologies:
- *101 Poems for Children: A Laureate's Choice* chosen by Carol Ann Duffy
- *Poetry for Kids: William Shakespeare* edited by Dr Marguerite Tassi
- *I Am the Seed That Grew the Tree: A nature poem for every day of the year* selected by Fiona Waters
- *Poetry for Young People* by Maya Angelou

Reflect on your learning in this chapter
- What techniques have you learned to improve your reading, speaking and listening and writing?
- Make a list of things that you still need to master – or concepts with which you need more practice.
  - Compile a plan for tackling these.
  - Discuss your lists and ideas with your classmates and your teacher.

Reading

★ A humorous play
★ A praise poem
★ A dramatic poem
★ A narrative poem

Speaking and listening

★ Delivering a speech for brighter future
★ Performing a poem

ALL THE WORLD'S A STAGE

Writing

★ A speech about an important issue
★ A short one-act play in a group
★ A movie or TV script

Key skills

★ Tone of voice and register

LET'S TALK

■ What is drama?

■ How do plays differ from short stories or novels?

■ What makes a good speech?

■ What jobs require good public speaking?

■ What movies or series have you watched that you think had excellent scripts? What made the scripts so good?

Speaking and listening

Organising a speech

Your teacher will play you an excerpt from a famous political speech.

The excerpt of the speech you will listen to was delivered on Wednesday, 29 August 1963 during a march on Washington and calls for the civil and economics right of African Americans.

Activity 9.1

In your groups, discuss the following questions:
1 What was the purpose of the speech?
2 Who is the audience?
3 What was the main idea or theme of the speech?
4 Why does Dr King repeat the 'I have a dream' line?
5 Explain why 'I have a dream' is more powerful than 'I hope ...'.
6 What is the tone and register of the monologue?
7 How has Dr King used emotive and persuasive language? Give an example of each kind.

Spotlight on: organisation
Did you notice the repeated phrase 'I have a dream'?
Martin Luther King uses this as a pattern to organise his speech. Whenever the audience hears the repeat, they know the next part of the argument is going to build.

EXERCISE 9.1
Listen again to the speech.

Make a visual organiser to track the argument.

Argument 1 → Argument 2 → Argument 3

Reading

Spotlight on: paragraphs

Paragraphs organise your writing into units to:

■ organise the flow of the writing
■ break the writing into chunks of meaning
■ help the reader understand what they are reading.

Organising ideas

In fiction, writers often begin a new paragraph when:

■ there is a change of time
■ there is a change of place
■ there is a change of viewpoint or character
■ there is a new action.

Activity 9.2

Select a fiction book or extract.
Look for paragraph changes.
Keep a tally chart to record why the writer has started a new paragraph.

Change of time	
Change of place	
Change of viewpoint or character	
New action	
Other	

Authors have new lines for new speakers in dialogue. Focus on descriptive passages for this exercise about paragraphs.

Activity 9.3

Look back through some of your own writing. For example, go back to your story episode from Chapter 6.

■ Did you use paragraphs to organise your writing?
■ Can you explain the decisions you made? Was it for a change of time, place or action?
■ If you did not use paragraphs, decide where you would break it up.

Writing

Write a speech

In non-fiction, writers begin a new paragraph:

- for an introduction or conclusion
- when there is a change of topic
- when the argument builds to a new stage
- when there is a change in argument – for example, changing from arguing for something, to giving an opinion against it.

Now let's think about using paragraphs to organise the thinking in a speech.

EXERCISE 9.2

Martin Luther King gave his speech because he hoped for change in the future.

Now you will write your own speech. Think about changes you would like to see for a better world and a brighter, fairer future for your generation and the generations to come.
Think about issues that are important to you.
Your goal is to write a speech that shares your vision, and that raises the spirits of your audience.

Plan your paragraphs like this.

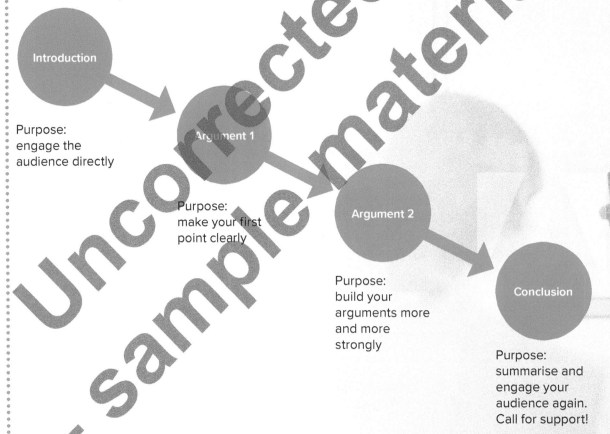

Introduction

Purpose: engage the audience directly

Argument 1

Purpose: make your first point clearly

Argument 2

Purpose: build your arguments more and more strongly

Conclusion

Purpose: summarise and engage your audience again. Call for support!

Organise your speech into paragraphs and use techniques such as repetition and powerful language to convince your audience.

Speaking

Speech performance

Now, you will perform your speech to the class. Use the following steps to help you prepare.

Step 1: Rehearse

You do not need to learn every word 'by heart'. However, you should become familiar with your speech by rehearsing.

Expert hint – Some speakers use cards to organise their speeches. They have a different card for each paragraph. These are called 'cue cards'. If you use cue cards, make sure you number them in case you drop them!

Step 2: Tone, voice and gesture

Think about the flow of your speech.
- Where should your voice be low or quiet or calm?
- Where should your voice raise or be powerful?
- What kinds of gestures could support different stages of your argument?

Make notes on your speech or on your cue cards to help.

Step 3: Feedback

Work with a partner or in a small group.

Listen and watch each other.

Give hints and tips for how to improve the speech.

> Practising with a small group will build your confidence.

Step 4: Perform

Perform your speech and listen to your classmates. Remember, good listeners will use eye contact and non-verbal gestures such as nodding to show they are listening. You can share your positive feedback with your classmates when they have finished their speech. If you think there is something your classmate could do to make their speech even better, remember to share your ideas sensitively and include what they did well.

Imbongi Bongani Sithole

Bongani Sithole (born 1937) grew up near Umtata in the Eastern Cape in South Africa. He worked for the University of the Transkei as a research assistant.

Performance poetry

This is an extract of a praise poem performed by the imbongi Bongani Sithole. An imbongi is a traditional praise poet. He sings the praises of important people. This type of performance poetry is always oral and is composed and performed spontaneously.

Extract: 'The praises of Nelson Rolihlahla Mandela'

Hail Dalibhunga!

Words of truth have been exposed.

He's the bull that kicks up dust and stones and breaks antheaps

He's the wild animal that stares at the sky

Until all the stars fall down

I say to you Dalibhunga

I say to you Madiba

I've done nothing, my countrymen

I remember you as a man when I saw you at Mfulo location in 1957

You and Slovo played hide and seek

Disguising yourself from people so that you shouldn't be identified

You are the Paramount Chief of the Thembus with the light complexion

The son of the princess of the Konjwayo's

A king born of the princess of the nation

A bright man of the woman of the nation

Someone who stamped his feet on the mountain of Mtata

And the whites became frightened

Someone who drank from the waters of the sea

Until the water dried up and only the stones were left.

A king who did wonderful things amongst different tribes

So that the Thembu house was shocked

It was said: 'What kind of a King is this?'

I've said nothing, Thembu people, I have said nothing.

Recorded, transcribed and translated by Russell H Kaschula

Dalibhunga was the name given to Mr Mandela at the age of 16 when he had undergone initiation – the traditional Xhosa rite of passage into manhood. It means 'creator of the council'.

Madiba is a clan name. It is more than a surname as it refers to the ancestor from whom a person is descended.

Spotlight on: political context

Political context refers to the state, government – the policies, laws and civil rights of people in a place or country at a specific time.

Activity 9.3

Listen to a recording of the poem. Can you hear the power of the performance and the way the speaker changes the tone and feeling in the voice? Read the poem aloud to one another. Try to use your voice in the same way, to bring power and feeling to the text.

LONG PAGE

EXERCISE 9.3

1   What is the purpose of this text? What is the main idea?

2   What are the incredible feats that the imbongi describes? Why does he do this? What is its effect?

3   Why does the imbongi repeat 'I've said nothing ... I have said nothing'?

4   How does the imbongi show bias?

Dramatic poetry

As you read this poem, think about how you could perform it.

Poet: Roger McGough

Roger McGough (born 1937) is an English poet, children's author and playwright.

1 Why does the poet repeat the sound here to form this nonsense word? What does it say about the speaker in the poem?

2 Why does the poet begin the stanza with a connective?

3 What is the effect of the alliteration and sibilance in these lines?

4 Does the poet expect an answer to these questions?

5 Why does the poet repeat the words railing and lessin?

6 What sound is repeated? What is its effect?

7 Why do you think the poet only used rhyme in the last two lines?

'First Day at School'

A millionbillionwillion miles from home
Waiting for the bell to go. (To go where?)
Why are they all so big, other children?
So noisy? So much at home they
Must have been born in uniform
Lived all their lives in playgrounds
Spent the years inventing games
That don't let me in. Games
That are rough, that swallow you up.

And the railings.
All around, the railings.
Are they to keep out wolves and monsters?
Things that carry off and eat children?
Things you don't take sweets from?
Perhaps they're to stop us getting out
Running away from the lessins. Lessin.
What does a lessin look like?
Sounds small and slimy.
They keep them in the glassrooms.
Whole rooms made out of glass. Imagine.

I wish I could remember my name
Mummy said it would come in useful.
Like wellies. When there's puddles.
Yellowwellies. I wish she was here.
I think my name is sewn on somewhere
Perhaps the teacher will read it for me.
Tea-cher. The one who makes the tea.

Roger McGough

EXERCISE 9.4

1 Choose three details mentioned by the child in 'First Day at School' that show that the child finds the school strange and rather scary and explain why.

2 Why do you think the words 'To go where?' in line 2 are put in brackets?

3 The child narrator is obviously confused and misunderstands some of the words that are used. Quote some of these misunderstandings, explain them and say how they help you to understand the child's confusion.

4 What impression does the poem give you of the school? In particular, think about the reference to the railings.

Activity 9.4

Now prepare a performance of the poem.
- Think especially about how to use your voice, gestures and facial expressions.
- Who is narrating the poem?
- How would they say the questions?
- Are they expecting answers?
- What are their hopes and fears?

Drama

Features of drama

Plays are written in a specific form, using a play script. The words the characters say (dialogue) are separated from their movements or gestures (stage directions). **Stage directions** are usually given in brackets and/or italics. They tell the actors how to move and make gestures and how to say a particular line.

Dialogue is the actual words that the actors say. The words are written next to the name of a character. A particularly long speech is called a monologue. At times, actors talk directly to the audience. This is known as an aside.

Plot: Plot in a drama works in the same way as in a novel or short story. However, sometimes the audience knows something that the characters do not. This is known as dramatic irony.

KEY WORDS

protagonist the main or central figure of a story

antagonist a character usually acting in conflict as a foil to the protagonist

characterisation the way that characters are represented in a story, book, film or play so that they seem real and natural

Conflict: As with a novel or short story, there is conflict between the **protagonist** and **antagonist**(s). In a tragedy, this conflict will often come from a character flaw that the protagonist has, such as pride or greed.

Acts and scenes: An act is a main part of a story, which is then broken down into smaller scenes. Some plays only have one act (known as a one-act play), while others may have as many as five acts. Scenes usually change when the set of characters or the location or setting changes.

The stage curtains usually close between acts. This gives the audience a break and allows the props or scenes on stage to be changed, if necessary.

Lights and sound effects: Many stage productions use lights and sound effects to improve the performance. A 'spot' is a light that may follow an actor around the stage. Sound effects or music are often added to make the play more realistic, for example by giving the background sounds such as a busy street to set the scene.

Costume and make-up: Actors usually wear costumes for their parts. Make-up is often done in an exaggerated way so that people sitting far away can see the actors' expressions more clearly. Costume adds to the **characterisation** of the actor.

Sets and props: A set is the physical backdrop (such as the walls of a room or the front of a boat) or something that is on the stage, like furniture. Props are the loose things that characters use, such as glasses, a tray, a mirror. These add realism to the play.

LET'S TALK

Discuss these questions in your groups and give feedback to the class.

- How do plays differ from movies or TV or radio dramas?
- What can you do in a movie or on television that you cannot do on stage?
- What can plays do that television dramas and movies cannot do?
- How do you think that the scripts for TV, movies or radio are different from play scripts?

Organisation of playscripts

Playscripts are written to tell the actors, director and stage managers what will happen on the stage.

This needs careful organisation. The following examples are from a humorous play set in the time of Vikings.

Character list

A play begins with a character list. This gives the necessary background information about the characters and the props or costumes needed.

Acts and scenes

Plays are organised into acts and scenes. These are like chapters in a fiction novel. If there is a change of place or time, there is a new scene.

Act 1, Scene 1

Setting: two scribes, wearing brown robes with large cowls are sitting at a large desk, writing out books with feather quills. There are candles on the side. Two large doors are on the right of the stage, just above the stairs.

ENTER NARRATOR.

The setting is described clearly and concisely. These words are not meant to be said by the actors, but they help the director know what the stage should look like.

Stage directions

These are quick notes that tell the actors when to enter or exit the stage, how to move or how to say the lines. These stage directions are often put in brackets. This means the actors can see them but they know not to say them to the audience.

Activity 9.5

Sketch a picture of how you would arrange the stage for this play. What atmosphere would you create for the audience as the curtain first rises?

Activity 9.6

1 Practise reading these lines with a partner.
REMEMBER – do not say the stage directions but use them to help you know how to say the lines and what to do!

SCRIBE 2: *(Thinking for a second)* Nope, it doesn't ring any bells!
SCRIBE 1: *(Frantically paging through their manuscripts)* Wait. Perhaps we have not transcribed that part yet. I told you to write faster and drink your meade slower.

2 There are five characters in the playscript. Work in a small group to read through the play together.
Think about how the characters would say the words, use gestures and move on stage. Remember not to read out the stage directions.

Activity 9.7

Read through this text in a small group. Take on different characters and read the play 'unseen': this means you will read it together first without a rehearsal. Practise reading slightly ahead, so you adapt your voice to the tone and meaning.

Extract: *How Norse words were introduced into the English language*

Character list

NARRATOR: a boy/girl dressed in a white robe

SCRIBE 1: a boy/girl dressed in a brown robe with cowl

SCRIBE 2: a boy/girl dressed in a brown robe with cowl

SAGA: a boy/girl Viking wearing a skirt or pants with a faux fur and a large book labelled 'DICTIONARY, under his or her arm

EEE: a boy/girl dressed similarly to SAGA with a plastic or paper axe or sword

Act 1, Scene 1

Setting: two scribes, wearing brown robes with large cowls are sitting at a large desk, writing out books with feather quills. There are candles on the side. Two large doors are on the right of the stage, just above the stairs.

ENTER NARRATOR.

NARRATOR: It is the year 793, the dawn of the Viking era. The Vikings prepare their first attack on Lindisfarne, a small monastery on an island off the northeast coast of England where two scribes are peacefully writing out manuscripts … But not for long! *(EXIT NARRATOR)*

A longboat pulls up on the shore of the steps of the stage. ENTER SAGA and EEE.

EEE: With this book I take your ignorance in the name of the mighty Oden.

SCRIBE 1: Who on earth is Oden?

SAGA: Oden is the son of Bor and the giantess Bestla. He is the king of Asgard – the father of all Norse Mythology.

SCRIBE 2: *(Thinking for a second)* Nope, it doesn't ring any bells!

SCRIBE 1: *(Frantically paging through their manuscripts)* Wait. Perhaps we have not transcribed that part yet. I told you to write faster and drink your meade slower.

EEE: Well, then, we will have to teach you about our language and culture.

SCRIBE 2: Don't be preposterous. We have nothing to learn from you!

SAGA: *(A bit sad)* But we have such good words in our dictionary!

SCRIBE 2: What is this 'DITCHINERY' of which you speak?

EEE: It is the greatest collection of words.

SCRIBE 1: Pah! These manuscripts are also full of beautiful, poetic words.

1 What can you tell about the setting of the play?

2 Why is this said by the narrator?

HINT
As you read through the play below, think about how the characters would say the words, use gestures and move on stage.

3 Explain the underlined simile.

4 What kind of play is this? how do you know?

5 How has the playwright created distinctive voices for the characters?

6 What is the main theme of the play?

7 Why are there ellipses here?

SAGA: No, a dictionary has lists of words with their meanings and their history. Look! *(He takes the dictionary from under his arm and opens it)* <u>It is like a hall of fame for words.</u>

EEE: *(Aside)* Yes, even the word 'Dictionary' is in there!

SCRIBE 2: What codswallop! Who would want a book of random words? I have never heard of such nonsense!

SAGA: *(Aside)* <u>These savages probably haven't invented dictionaries yet.</u> *(To the scribes)* Words are like swords – they are powerful. We have proud Viking words like 'pillage' and 'plunder'.

SCRIBE 1: We also have the word 'village' and what is this 'plunder' of which you speak.

EEE: Plunder is … *(He looks up the word)* when you send warriors to take money and things from people in the villages.

SCRIBE 1: *(Chuckling and nudging SCRIBE 2)* Oh, we have a phrase for that: tax collecting!

The Vikings look at each other, quite confused.

EEE: And there is 'blunder'. *(Closes his eyes, and walks into the table, making a loud and exaggerated 'OW')* See, that is 'blunder'.

SCRIBE 2: *(To Scribe 1)* I think he is talking about the effects of meade!

SAGA: Well, anyway, there are many good words from Old Norse, like 'happ' which means good fortune. *(He fakes a big smile)* See this is 'Happ'. How would you act out the word 'Happ' EEE?

EEE: It means this. *(He fakes a big smile – and points to the corners of his mouth to exaggerate it)*

SCRIBE: Happ-EEE! Aaah. Yet another word for meade.

SAGA: Comparing our words to meade? How dare you show such disrespect!

EEE: Unsheath your sword, SAGA, and let us show these sorry excuses for scholars some respect! Prepare thyself to die by the sword then!

SCRIBE 1: No, no … *(He picks up the skirt of his robe in an exaggerated way and runs with little steps)*

EXIT SCRIBE 1.

SAGA: 'Tis better to stand and fight, else you will die tired!

SCRIBE 2: HELPPPP! Dial 911! *(Aside)* Now, those are powerful English words!

EXIT SCRIBE 2 runs away holding his skirt too.

EEE and SAGA EXIT after them. There are the sounds of swords clanging backstage.

EEE: *(Voice drifts in from offstage)* I told you, Saga, next time just knock on the door and leave a copy of the dictionary on the doorstep. It's been working wonders for the people who deliver telephone directories.

Reading

Playwright: Justin Gray

Justin Gray is a South African accounting student and author. He has published a fantasy novel.

As you read the play below, think about the tone of voice and register that each actor will use.

Extract: *In Search of Jerome Jiggins*

Character list

CONSTABLE COLLINS: a tall thin boy/girl dressed as a police constable in a police uniform and hat

WILD WILL: a boy wearing a cowboy hat and cowboy boots

KNIGHT STEWART: a boy wearing a robe with a robe and a cardboard or plastic sword hanging from his belt

DAMSEL DANIELLA: a girl wearing a long dress and cone hat with a sash hanging from it

Scene 1

A police station with a high reception desk and a large wooden desk in a small police station. There is a huge pile of paper marked IN.

ENTER CONSTABLE COLLINS.

Constable Collins: (*Quite exhausted, walking to his desk*) Oh it never-ever-ever-ever ends! Non-stop paperwork (*gesturing to the IN pile*) and pointless calls! (*Mimicking a whiney voice as he picks up the phone at his desk*) 'My cat is stuck in a tree, Constable Sir!', 'My neighbour won't stop playing opera while I play my hip-hop and it is such an inconvenience to me!', 'My mum says I am grounded but I have a sleepover to go to! What do I do, Constable Sir Officer?' I will tell you what to do – bother some other poor sad sack! I just wish the Constabulary started meaning something again! Oh! I miss it all, the robberies, the chases and all the mighty praise!

ENTER WILD WILL dragging a dog's lead with an empty collar, KNIGHT STEWARD and DAMSEL DANIELLA through the Constabulary doors; all three breathing from exhaustion.

CONSTABLE COLLINS stands instantly to attention.

CONSTABLE COLLINS: Good afternoon, this is the Calloway Constabulary. What issue may I help –

1 What does this monologue tell us about the Constable's character?

2 Why has the playwright used a semi-colon and not a full stop after 'doors'?

3 Why does the playwright use non-standard English? What do words such as 'whippersnapper' say about this character?

4 Why does Knight Stewart call the Constable 'Sir'?

5 How effective is the underlined simile?

7 Why does the playwright choose these words?

8 What is the effect of all these short questions?

9 Is the stage direction needed here? Why?

10 What information does Constable Collins *not* ask for?

11 How effective are the similes?

WILD WILL: Shut yer yapper, whippersnapper! We need us the local lawman, the one what does all the lawmanning. So, go get 'im then!

KNIGHT STEWART: (*Coughing audibly and to Will*) Good friend, William, this whippersnapper does so happen to be the very man of laws we seek. (*To the Constable, he bows*) Good day, Noble Sir. We have an issue, and you are the great and daring champion we –

DAMSEL DANIELLA: A tragedy! An outright tragedy! Oh, how terrible! Our dear friend –

WILD WILL: Oh, put a can in it, Daniella! Cats waffle on less than you and I speak to cats on the regular! (*To the Constable*) So, you the voice of the Law, huh? (*Aside, in a low whisper*) Not much is he, eh Dox? He be built like a blade of dried grass …

CONSTABLE COLLINS: (*Confused*) Who is he talking to?

DAMSEL DANIELLA: (*Fluttering a makeshift paper fan*) Oh I told him not to bring his dog, I just did! That dreadful creature makes more noise than footballers on game night! Doggone Dox I call that Dog!

CONSTABLE COLLINS: (*Aside*) I should have gone into writing; I don't get paid nearly enough for any of this!

KNIGHT STEWART: Lady and Gentlemen, please, collect yourselves at once! Our friend's livelihood is at risk here! And it only gets worse the more we dilly dally on nonsense. We must inform our noble champion of our urgent quest!

6 Why did the playwright use a semi-colon here?

WILD WILL: The knight has a point there. Listen, lawman, our friend's missing, stolen by some Ruddy Rascal of a Ruffian and we need you, our 'Champion' to go and unpickle this pickle. You understand?

CONSTABLE COLLINS: Your friend was stolen you say? Actually stolen? This is not a joke? A prank?

KNIGHT STEWART: (*Shocked, hand to his chest*) Whosoever would make such a cruel jest of such a horrendous evil? Our friend was stolen, Noble Champion, and we cannot embark upon such a quest without you! To do so would be against the written laws of this land and those we cannot break!

DAMSEL DANIELLA: Oh, will you help, man? Will you?

WILD WILL: (*Crossing his arms, looking away, sulkily*) I'd not need your help if it weren't for the world changing. Man can't do no good deed without approval from the law, otherwise I'd have my peashooters singling out this ruffian. So, whadya say, bucko?

CONSTABLE COLLINS: (*Sighing*) Give me details first. Age, height, physical appearance and anything else that could be considered important.

WILD WILL: (*Scoffing*) Well, he's as scrawny as a rancher's scarecrow and as shaky as a chicken at feeding time, with ears the size of an elephant and the teeth of a hamster.

12 How do the different character's descriptions change according to their distinctive voice?

KNIGHT STEWART: With hair as dark as the darkest night and a voice as clear and beautiful as the Lady of the Lake herself.

DAMSEL DANIELLA: And the ocean's eyes and a kitten's soft feet and wittle wabbit's nose and a heart of Gold, centuries old!

CONSTABLE COLLINS: *(Writing down notes)* Right, age?

KNIGHT STEWART: Eleven summer's old!

13 Is this formal or informal language? Why does the Constable use it even when he is addressing children?

CONSTABLE COLLINS: *(Confused)* I beg your pardon?

DAMSEL DANIELLA: *(Shaking her hands in frustration)* YEARS, Constable sir, they mean YEARS, now is not the time to be dummies, boys!

CONSTABLE COLLINS: Eleven … years … Right, now where did you see him get kidnapped?

DAMSEL DANIELLA: Oh dear, right there by Wendy's Way! Oh, don't look so confused, Constable dear, where the school is!

CONSTABLE COLLINS: Ah yes, of course, Wendyville Avenue! Right, I will file a missing person's report and I will contact you once any progress is made, children.

ALL OF THEM: *(Yelling)* NO!

WILD WILL: You do that, they'll know we ratted on them. The infamous Enigmatic Gang always know, and then they'll hurt our pal and this will just be one big waste!

CONSTABLE COLLINS: Enigmatic Gang? That's ridiculous! I've never heard of them!

KNIGHT STEWART: Why, that's the thing, you don't know them because enigmas aren't meant to be known, brave Constable. We can only do this if you help us directly. Will you, Constable Sir?

CONSTABLE COLLINS: *(Aside)* It's just children being children … But so what? A missing person is a missing person and it's my job to find them and bring the perpetrators to justice. *(To the children)* Let's go restore law and order to this town!

ALL OF THEM: *(Jumping up and down)* Hooray! Hooray! Hooray!

WILD WILL: Just one catchy catch catch there – only us three can see our friend and the Enigmatic Gang.

14 Why are there ellipses used here?

CONSTABLE COLLINS: Wait … Let me get this straight … do you mean to say that both the victim and the perpetrators are – *imaginary?*

DAMSEL DANIELLA: *(Aside)* By Jove, the Constable's got it – and here I thought he was a bit slow!

15 What is the purpose of the dash?

WILD WILL: *(Shy)* Uh … yes … Sir. But it would mean a lot to us if you could help. I would really appreciate it if you could scare him with the law.

CONSTABLE COLLINS: How very formal of you, Son!

WILD WILL: Hey! I read me some books!

Justin Gray

Key skills

Tone of voice and register

Tone of voice is the emotion or mood that characters show in their voice to communicate their feelings and enhance meaning. Register refers to how friendly (informal) or formal the language is that the actors or characters use. Characters or actors can also change the pace of their voice (for example, speaking faster when they are excited and slower when they are confused) or volume (for example, speaking louder when they are angry, excited or happy, and softer when they are sad).

EXERCISE 9.5

1 Take each character/actor and make notes on the tone of voice and register you think they will use at various points in the scene.
2 Perform these examples as you think they will be said for your class or group.

Activity 9.8

1 How does the playwright create distinctive voices for each character? Comment on the following:
   - Make-up and costume
   - The props
   - The language (dialogue) in the script
   - The non-verbal language such as movement, facial expressions and gestures
   - How the actor says the lines: the pace (how fast or slow), tone of voice and register (formal or informal)
2 Did you like the play? Why or why not?

EXTENSION
What do you think happens next? In pairs, or a small group, write Scene 2. Think about the words each character will use.

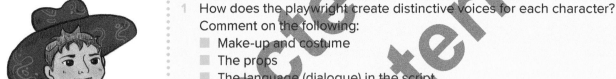

Writing

Activity 9.9

As a group, write a short one-act play. Here are some ideas:
- A bully or criminal who gets outwitted
- A modern take on a well-known folk tale
- A detective agency that takes on a new and interesting case

You can find many templates online to use as the basis for planning a play. You could also use a storyboard or mind map.

Follow the steps given on the writing cycle on page v.

When you write your play, remember to:
- Use the correct writing conventions for play scripts.
- Give each actor a distinctive voice. Think about the words they will use, the gestures or movements they will make, the props they will need and how they will interact with other characters.

Activity 9.10

Having had the chance to write a play as a group, you now get the chance to write your own script for a movie or TV show. Although you will only be writing a single scene, you need to think about the whole play.
- What type of movie or TV show is it? Who is the audience/viewers? How will they relate to the characters/actors? Which movies or TV shows are similar to this? How will yours be different? What language will you use to create each character and to give them a distinctive voice?

- What location (setting), props and costumes do you need?
- How can you use more interesting adjectives, adverbs and connectives to make your language more interesting?

EXTENSION

If possible, film and edit your scene. (You will be the writer and director.) Ask other learners to be the actors. Coach them and give them directions about how to portray your characters. Show your film to the class.

Give other learners constructive feedback on their films.

Reviewing

Reflect on the speeches, plays and dramatic poems you've read in this chapter

Talk about:
- which texts you liked and which you didn't like
- which you think were well-written and why
- your favourite speeches from your classmates. Which one did you enjoy the most?
- how you found writing a play in a group compared to writing a film script/TV show alone. Which form of writing did you prefer?

If you enjoyed reading these plays, then try the following:
- *Much Ado about Nothing* by William Shakespeare
- *The Importance of Being Earnest* by Oscar Wilde
- *Harry Potter and the Cursed Child* by JK Rowling, John Tiffany and Jack Thorne
- *The Curious Incident of the Dog in the Night Time* by Mark Haddon, Simon Stephens, Paul Bunyan, Ruth Moore
- *A Raisin in the Sun* by Lorraine Hansberry

LET'S TALK

Talk about what great new skills you have learned.

Reflect on your learning in this chapter
- What new skills and techniques have you learned to improve your reading, speaking and listening and writing?
- Make a list of things that you still need to master – or concepts with which you need more practice.
  - Compile a plan for tackling these.
  - Discuss your lists and ideas with a partner and your teacher.

Glossary

adjective a word that is used to describe a noun, e.g. the *red* house

adverb a word, frequently ending in *-ly*, that is used to describe the action expressed by a verb, e.g. Joe ate *hungrily.*

alliteration the repetition of consonant sounds at the beginning of words

antagonist a character usually acting in conflict or as a foil to the protagonist

anthology a published collection of writing, usually of poems or short stories

atmosphere how the physical situation or environment feels

apostrophe a punctuation mark (') indicating possession or omission

assonance the repetition of the same or similar vowel sounds within words, phrases or sentences

audience the people for whom authors have written their work

autobiography a true story about someone's life, told by that person

ballads poems that tell stories, sometimes set to music

characterisation the way that characters are represented in a story, book, film or play so that they seem real and natural

clause a group of words containing a verb. A *main* clause makes sense on its own; a *subordinate* clause depends on a main clause for its sense to be clear

complex sentence a long sentence consisting of interlinked main and subordinate clauses and phrases

compound sentence a sentence consisting of two or more main clauses linked by coordinating conjunctions

connective any word that links clauses, sentences or ideas together

culture a particular way of life, including the customs and traditions, beliefs, knowledge and behaviours of a particular group of people at a particular time

direct speech the words actually spoken by someone, indicated by speech marks ('...')

emotive language words chosen by writers deliberately to arouse feelings in their readers

enjambment a term used to describe lines of poetry that run on from one line to the next without a pause

factual information information that is accurate and true. This can be found in texts such as textbooks, encyclopedias, recipes and timetables

first-person narrative (using 'I') telling the story from one of the character's point of view

folk tales stories that are handed down from generation to generation, usually in spoken form

free verse a poem with no fixed or regular structure

genre a particular type of literature or other art form, e.g. novel, poetry, science fiction

inverted commas the same as speech marks or quotation marks, mainly used for direct speech, quotations or titles

lyrical (non-narrative) poem a poem about a particular experience, usually showing strong feelings in a short form

metre the regular recurring rhythmic pattern of stressed and unstressed syllables on which a poem is based

modal verbs 'helping' verbs or auxiliary verbs such as *can, may, will, could, should, would, shall, must, ought to* and *might.* They add meaning to the main verb in a sentence as they add possibility, ability, permission or obligation

mood the emotional setting; the feeling a reader gets when reading a poem

narrative poem a poem that tells a story

noun a word that gives the name of a person, place, thing or abstract idea

novel a work of fiction, usually written in a book

omniscient approach the narrator knows the thoughts and feelings of all of the characters in the story

onomatopoeia when the sound of a word echoes its meaning, e.g. *boom*

oral storytelling a story in spoken form

paragraph a group of closely related sentences that develop a central or main idea

personality what a person's character and behaviour are like

phrase a group of words that do not contain a verb, e.g. She ate her breakfast *while on the bus*.

prose a form of communication that uses ordinary grammar and flow

protagonist the main or central figure of a story

purpose the reason or intention for writing the piece, e.g. to amuse, to inform, to entertain

register how friendly (informal) or formal the language is that the characters use

repetition to repeat words or phrases again and again

rhyme when the endings of two or more words sound alike, e.g. *lean* and *seen*

rhyme scheme the pattern of sounds that repeats at the end of a line or stanza (verse)

rhythm the pattern of beats in a poem or a sentence

script the written text of a video, play, movie or book

sentence opener the first word or phrase used in a sentence

setting the place or places in which the events occur

sibilance the repetition of the `s' sound or `sh' or `ch' sounds

simile a figure of speech in which two things that are not obviously like each other are compared to make a description more vivid. A simile will often begin with a phrase introduced by 'like' or 'as', e.g. *The smoke hung from the chimney like a drooping flag.*

simple sentence a sentence with only one independent clause

sonnet a form of poem that always has 14 lines

speech marks (' ') punctuation marks to indicate the beginning and end of direct speech

stanza a verse in a poem which is made up of two or more lines, which often have a common rhyme and pattern

structure the way a text is organised so that it usually has a beginning, middle and end

syllable a unit of sound (a beat) that can be a word on its own, e.g. *man*; but can be joined with other units of sound to form words, e.g. *woman*

synonyms words that have similar meanings

theme the content of a text: what a text is about

third person narrative (using 'he', 'she', etc.) the writer shows the thoughts and feelings of several characters

tone what the author feels or wants the reader to feel about something. Tone can be humorous, dark or angry, for example

topic sentence a sentence that contains the main topic or summary of the paragraph. It is usually the first sentence in a paragraph

verb a word that expresses an action or a state of being, e.g. Joe *ate* his dinner. Joe no longer *felt* hungry

voice an author's unique style of writing